"How long we have waited for a book like this! It has been a generation or two since such a work on such a vital theme has been produced. And the church shows it. Dr. Olford has presented truth that can revolutionize churches and individuals. We will learn 'not I, but Christ,' or we will continue in decline and spiritual degeneration. I would that every true believer would earnestly read this book and live by its timeless biblical truths."

—LEWIS B. DRUMMOND, Billy Graham Professor of Evangelism
and Church Growth, Beeson Divinity School

"Not I, But Christ simply and effectively expounds the profound 'secret' to living the Christian life so powerfully summarized by Paul in Galatians 2:20. If even a small minority of American Christians were to read and heed this book, we would have the greatest spiritual awakening in the history of our country.

"Warmly illustrated with personal anecdotes, stories from the lives of great Christians ancient and modern, and powerful biblical examples, Stephen Olford's message is desperately needed by American Christians on the brink of the twenty-first century.

"While many believe we live in an age in which Christians are nontheological, Stephen Olford disagrees. He has captured the classic evangelical doctrine of sanctification and expressed it for a new generation in this most personal new work."

—KENDELL H. EASLEY, Associate Professor of New Testament and Greek,
Mid-America Baptist Theological Seminary

"This excellent book is a distillation of Dr. Stephen Olford's many years of ministry—a crystallization of the biblical truth that has not only shaped his thinking but empowered his life. In it Dr. Olford, with the eloquence typical of his preaching, has shared the open secret of victorious living: it is not a philosophy to be learned, nor deeper doctrinal insight to be grasped; it is not some new spiritual discipline to be practiced, but the simple yet profound reality that the risen Lord Jesus Christ wishes to live out His life through ordinary men and women by the power of His Holy Spirit who resides within them. The message of this book has the potential of radically changing those who read it as well as the church to which they belong, for it is not just an interesting theory to be questioned, but a fact that has been demonstrated to be true by the life of its author. It is a message we all need to hear and heed!"

—GERALD F. HAWTHORNE, Professor of Greek, Wheaton College

"Making the Apostle Paul's testimony his own, Dr. Olford shows us how Galatians 2:20 contains the essentials of the Christian life. Here is truth aflame with clarity and conviction. If 'Christianity is Christ,' then this powerful book is a splendid commentary on that truth."

—TED S. RENDALL, Chancellor, Prairie Bible Institute

"With spiritual insight and penetrating skills, Stephen Olford goes right to the core of biblical Christianity. In this day when human effort often passes for spiritual zeal, this is a welcome, penetrating, and vital book."

—ADRIAN ROGERS, Pastor, Bellevue Baptist Church, Cordova, TN

"Dr. Olford has caught the absolute necessity for the centrality of the cross in the believer's life in his excellent treatment of Galatians 2:20. This book is must reading for all pastors who would minister to the deepest needs of their people and for believers who are serious about their spiritual growth."

—CHARLES R. SOLOMON, Founder and President, Grace Fellowship Intl.

"Dr. Stephen Olford has not only been my mentor as an expository preacher of the gospel, but also a very special friend to me as a pastor. The message 'not I, but Christ' I know to be the message of his life and the truth that needs to be sounded in every pulpit in the world. Herein is the clearest explanation of this essential truth of the Christian life to be found anywhere. When you read it, anticipate a fresh new examination of every area of your walk with God."

—CHARLES F. STANLEY, Pastor, First Baptist Church, Atlanta, GA

Not I, But Christ

Not I, But Christ

Stephen F. Olford

CROSSWAY BOOKS • WHEATON, ILLINOIS
A DIVISION OF GOOD NEWS PUBLISHERS

Not I, But Christ

Copyright © 1995 by Stephen F. Olford

Published by Crossway Books
    a division of Good News Publishers
    1300 Crescent Street
    Wheaton, Illinois 60187

Unless otherwise indicated in the text, the majority of Scripture quotations used in this publication are taken from the *The Holy Bible, New King James Version*. Copyright © 1979, 1980, 1982 by Thomas Nelson, Inc., Publishers, Nashville, Tennessee.

Scripture quotations taken from the *New Revised Standard Version* are identified NRSV. Copyright © 1989 by the Division of Christian Education of the National Council of Churches in the USA. Published by Oxford University Press, New York.

Scripture taken from the Holy Bible: *New International Version®* is identified NIV. Copyright © 1973, 1978, 1984 by International Bible Society. Used by permission of Zondervan Publishing House. All rights reserved.

The "NIV" and "New International Version" trademarks are registered in the United States Patent and Trademark Office by International Bible Society. Use of either trademark requires the permission of International Bible Society.

Material taken from *The Christ-Life for the Self-Life* by F. B. Meyer, n.d.; from *Journals of John Wesley* edited by Percy L. Parker, 1974; from *The Wycliffe Bible Commentary* edited by Charles F. Pfeiffer and Everett F. Harrison, 1962; from *Five "Musts" of the Christian Life* by F. B. Meyer, 1927— copyright Moody Bible Institute of Chicago. Moody Press. Used by permission.

Material taken from *Expository Commentary on Hebrews* by J. C. Macaulay. Copyright © 1948 by J. C. Macaulay. Moody Press (ed. 1978). Used by permission.

Cover design: Cindy Kiple

First printing 1995

Printed in the United States of America

Library of Congress Cataloging-in-Publication Data
Olford, Stephen F.
   Not I, but Christ / Stephen F. Olford.
     p.   cm.
   Includes bibliographical references and index.
   1. Bible. N.T. Galatians II, 20—Commentaries. 2. Christian life—Biblical teaching. 3. Christian life—Baptist authors. I. Title.
BS2685.3.044 1995   227'.406—dc20   94-41421
ISBN 0-89107-801-0

03		02		01		00		99		98		97		96		95
15	14	13	12	11	10	9	8	7	6	5	4	3	2	1

Soli Deo gloria

Contents

Contents

Foreword

NOTHING IS MORE CENTRAL TO THE CHRISTIAN faith than the cross of Jesus Christ. And yet—as Stephen Olford points out in this eloquent and timely book—nothing is more neglected or misunderstood by many Christians today.

The cross of Christ is the foundation for our salvation, for (as the Apostle Paul wrote) Christ came from the Father "to reconcile to himself all things, whether things on earth or things in heaven, by making peace through his blood, shed on the cross" (Col. 1:20, NIV).

But the cross of Christ also is the foundation of our lives as believers, for God's plan was that through the cross our old nature would be crucified, and the power of the Holy Spirit would be unleashed to change our hearts and lives. Drawing on his deep understanding of this profound biblical truth, Stephen Olford explores in this book these dimensions of the cross and their practical meaning for our daily lives.

Few friends have meant as much to me across the years as Stephen Olford, and there are few preachers and Bible teachers I respect as highly. I first heard him preach in 1946 when I was visiting Great Britain with Youth for Christ. Later we spent time in Wales, searching the Word of God together and exploring many of the themes he sets forth in this volume. Across the years our continuing fellowship has been a source of blessing and encouragement to me and my associates.

I am grateful he has put these studies on the meaning of the cross of Christ into a book so they can have wider circulation. Biblical, balanced, and practical, it is a message sorely needed in our time. No reader can ponder its truth without being challenged and changed.

—BILLY GRAHAM

Acknowledgments

My special thanks:

To a host of preachers who have impacted my life and influenced my understanding of "the Christ-life for the self-life."

To my son David and other colleagues who have read the proofs and offered helpful corrections and suggestions.

To my beloved friend Billy Graham who has graciously written the Foreword.

To my devoted wife, Heather, whose encouragement and example have inspired the writing of the book.

To my homiletical secretary, Victoria Kuhl, who has edited and typed the manuscript.

And, finally, to my Savior and Lord, whose indwelling presence and power have made victorious living a glorious reality.

"I thank my God upon every remembrance of you" (Phil. 1:3).

Introduction

YEARS IN THE MINISTRY HAVE TAUGHT ME THAT many people endure the Christian life rather than enjoy it. They know what it is to be forgiven for their sins. They have the hope of heaven. But in between that initial experience of saving faith and that final experience of seeing Jesus there is a vast gap characterized by barrenness, frustration, and failure.

Even our churches reflect the shallow "easy believism" of our contemporary age. Thousands come through the front doors while tens of thousands leave through the back doors. According to British demographer David B. Barrett, editor of *World Christian Encyclopedia: A Comparative Study of Churches and Religion in the Modern World A.D. 1900-2000,* "more than 53,000 people leave church every week and never come back."[1] Disillusioned with programs and structures, they search for spirituality outside organized religion. And Dean M. Kelley, author of the book *Why Conservative Churches Are Growing,* contends that "conservative churches are 'growing' all right—but not through conversion growth. Most of it [comes through] babies and transfers."[2] Instead of preaching the message of a living, reigning, and caring Lord who is totally adequate for every human need, many men behind our pulpits have watered down the truth of the grace of God, thus giving reign to licentiousness and antinomianism.

Only God can reverse this trend by a heaven-sent revival. If His people will "humble themselves, and pray and seek [His] face, and turn from their wicked ways, then [and then alone—He] will hear from heaven, and will forgive their sin and heal their land" (2 Chron. 7:14). Revival, however, is not a gimmick; revival is God revealed in Christ and released by His Holy Spirit in power and "times of refreshing" and renewal. The need of the hour is a return to the core of our gospel, which is "Christ in [us], the hope of glory" (Col. 1:27).

Few verses in Scripture sum up this core message like Galatians 2:20: "I have been crucified with Christ; it is no longer I who live, but Christ lives in me; and the life which I now live in the flesh I live by faith in the Son of God, who loved me and gave Himself for me." So many Christians today try to live the Christian life apart from Christ; but such human endeavors are doomed to failure. Jesus made that clear when He declared with categorical finality: "Without Me you can do nothing" (John 15:5). Tragically, Christians still attempt to copy the Christ of history in their own strength.

The fact is, only *one* person ever lived the *Christian life;* it was Jesus, and He did so to the pleasure and glory of His Father (Luke 3:21-22; 9:28-35). Having fleshed out the perfect life in undeviating obedience to the will of God, "He became the author of eternal salvation to all who obey Him" (Heb. 5:9). After effecting that eternal salvation through the blood of His cross and the power of His resurrection, He ascended to heaven to impart His life, through the Holy Spirit, to all who believe His gospel and receive His full salvation. So the Christian life is nothing less than "the outliving of the indwelling Christ" on the principle of dependent faith. The Apostle Paul sums it up in the words that are the theme and thrust of this book: "I have been crucified with Christ; it is no longer I who live, but Christ lives in me; and the life which I now live in the flesh I live by faith in the Son of God, who loved me and gave Himself for me" (Gal. 2:20).

The miracle of the indwelling life of Christ is made possible by the power of the Holy Spirit. This truth will be developed more extensively in chapter 6. Suffice it to say at this point that the New Testament often equates the indwelt life of Christ with the indwelling work of the Spirit. Dr. Gordon D. Fee succinctly points this out in his impressive book, *God's Empowering Presence*. He writes:

> "Christ lives in me" . . . most likely is a kind of shorthand for "Christ by his Spirit lives in me." This is not to suggest that . . . the risen Lord and the Spirit are the same; rather, since the Spirit is indeed the Spirit *of Christ*, Pauline usage depends on the emphasis in a given context. Here [Gal. 2:20] the emphasis is on Christ and his work; hence he speaks of the indwelling Christ, rather than of the indwelling Spirit.[3]

No one, to my knowledge, has dealt so effectively with this tandem truth as Gerald F. Hawthorne in his book, *The Presence and the Power*. Writings like this are hard to come by in the literature of our day. Hawthorne admits that this "study [was] a long time aborning" (p. 1). But in the spring of 1991 he published his book, and it is now available for all to read. And it is a *must* for every Christian. His main thesis is that Jesus demonstrated His perfect humanity by His total faith-dependence on His Heavenly Father through the power of the Holy Spirit for His life and ministry. Hawthorne writes: "The story of the New Testament is not only the story of Jesus; it is also the story of the Holy Spirit in the lives of Jesus' followers" (p. 2). He goes on to say:

> Jesus was a genuine human being in the fullest sense of this term, hemmed in by the limits of his humanity. But he was a human being filled with the Spirit, the Spirit who on more than one occasion enabled Jesus to break through those human limits that bound him, so that the otherwise impossible became possible.
>
> Now what is of extraordinary importance to women and men today, people of all ages and from every country and social strata, is this: The very first thing Jesus did immediately after he was resurrected from among the dead and reunited with his followers was to pass on to them, as a gift from his Father (cf. Acts 2:23), that same power by which he lived, triumphed, and broke the bands of his own human limitations. On the very day of his resurrection, he came to them locked in by their fears, "breathed" (*enephysēse*) on them and said, "Receive the Holy Spirit" (John 20:22). . . .
>
> As it was true of Jesus, so it is true of his followers: "As the Father has sent me, even so I send you" (John 20:21b). As

Jesus was filled and equipped by the Spirit, so those who belong to Jesus are filled and equipped by the Spirit (Acts 2:4), or at least potentially so (Eph. 5:18). Just as it was true that this filling of Jesus enabled him to be and do the extraordinary, so it is true of those who believe in him.

The Acts of the Apostles (or "of the Holy Spirit"), to say the very least, was intended to show something of the nature of those things that God is able to do through people who yield themselves willingly to the influence of the Spirit. Through the Spirit those people of the very early church were enabled to preach boldly, convincingly, and authoritatively (Acts 2:14–41), to face crises and surmount obstacles with a courage and resoluteness and power they never dreamed they had (4:29-31), to cheerfully face persecution and suffering, and even to accept death with a prayer of forgiveness (5:40-41; 7:55-60), to heal the sick and raise the dead (9:36-41; 28:8), to arbitrate differences and bring about peace (15:1-35), to know where to go and where not to go, what to do and what not to do (16:6-10; 21:10-11), and so on. There is no reason whatsoever to believe that what was true of those earliest Christians is any less true of Christians in this century.[4] [See also Appendix A.]

I also commend to your reading Dr. V. Raymond Edman's little book, *They Found the Secret.* It has had a profound impact on me and many others worldwide because of the powerful examples of ordinary men and women who discovered "the Christ-life for the self-life." Some of those testimonies are included in chapter 1. But it is Edman's Conclusion to the book that provides a fitting introduction here to all that follows. Speaking of the essential stages of the life that wins, he writes:

> First, there is an *awareness* of our need, as expressed by the Lord Jesus, "If any man thirst . . ." (John 7:37). In similar vein the psalmist prayed: " . . . my soul thirsteth for thee, my flesh longeth for thee in a dry and thirsty land, where no water is; To see thy power and thy glory . . ." (Ps. 63:1–2).
>
> Then there is *agony* of soul because of that awareness. One remembers the beatitude: "Blessed are they which do hunger and thirst after righteousness: for they shall be filled" (Matt. 5:6). Hunger and thirst are not happy experiences, but they lead to true happiness. Crucifixion is a most painful process, and the soul that longs for fullness of life in Christ finds that the doorway to it is death to self. The Scriptures declare plainly: "They that are Christ's have crucified the flesh with the affections and lusts" (Gal. 5:24). It may seem that agony of soul is beyond endurance, but beyond it one comes to the glorious realization described in Galatians 2:20: "I am crucified with Christ: nevertheless I live: yet not I, but Christ liveth in me: and the life which I now live in the flesh I live by the faith of the Son of God, who loved me, and gave himself for me."
>
> Then follows wholehearted, unreserved *abandonment* to the Savior. Sick of self and sin, we obey the clear injunction of Romans 6:13: " . . . yield yourselves unto God, as those that are alive from the dead, and your members as instruments of righteousness unto God." Thereby Romans 12:1–2 becomes a living word to us: "I beseech you therefore, brethren, by the mercies of God, that ye present your bod-

ies a living sacrifice, holy, acceptable unto God, which is your reasonable service. And be not conformed to this world: but be ye transformed by the renewing of your mind, that ye may prove what is that good, and acceptable, and perfect, will of God."

Life, however, is not achieved by longing for a better life and lingering at the cross. There must be *appropriation* by faith of the Holy Spirit to fill life with the presence of the Lord Jesus. That obtainment is by faith, and not by works. Inquires the Scripture: "This only would I learn of you, Received ye the Spirit by the works of the law, or by the hearing of faith?" (Gal. 3:2). Just as salvation is by faith, so also is the exchanged life. Just as we accept the Lord Jesus by faith as Savior, so by simple faith we receive the fullness of the Holy Spirit. Just as we took the Lord as our sin-bearer, we take the Holy Spirit as our burden-bearer. Just as we take the Savior as our penalty for sins that are past, we take the Holy Spirit for power over indwelling sins that are present. The Savior is our atonement, the Holy Spirit is our advocate. In salvation we receive newness of life, by the Holy Spirit we find life more abundant. In each case the appropriation is by faith, and by faith alone, wholly apart from any feeling on our part.

Following appropriation there is *abiding* by faith in the Savior. Did He not say: "Abide in me, and I in you. As the branch cannot bear fruit of itself, except it abide in the vine; no more can ye, except ye abide in me. I am the vine, ye are the branches: He that abideth in me, and I in him, the same bringeth forth much fruit: for without me ye can do nothing" (John 15:4-5)? Abiding is obedience to His will. Declares 1 John 3:24: "And he that keepeth his commandments dwelleth in him, and he in him. And hereby we know that he abideth in us, by the Spirit which he hath given us." Abiding is not striving nor struggling, learned Hudson Taylor, but a resting in the Faithful One and implicit obedience to Him. The surrendered life that abides is a life of surrender.

The exchanged life is one of *abundance*. The Savior promised "rivers of living water" to flow from the Spirit-filled life (John 7:38). There is provision for life more abundant (John 10:10). And that life is indeed one of constant adventure, for it learns the wonderful reality of John 10:4: "And when he putteth forth his own sheep, he goeth before them, and the sheep follow him: for they know his voice." Who knows where He will lead and what He will say? Ear is tender to hear His voice, and heart is [set] on what the Altogether Lovely One will do. And that life can be yours and mine![5]

So I invite you to share with me some insights on the theme of "not I, but Christ." The chapter headings are as follows:

Not I, But Christ

Not I, But Christ and His Death

Not I, But Christ and His Life

Not I, But Christ and His Faith

Not I, But Christ and His Love

Not I, But Christ and His Grace

These studies were initially delivered to seminarians and pastors, but their message is essential and exciting for *every* Christian. The first and last chapters are simple expositions; the remaining four are more topical in treatment since they deal with the dominant aspects of the death of Christ, the life of Christ, the faith of Christ, and the love of Christ—as found in Galatians 2:20.

My earnest prayer is that as you peruse these pages, you will know in reality the truth expressed by Daniel W. Whittle:

Dying with Jesus by death reckoned mine,
Living with Jesus a new life divine,
Looking to Jesus till glory doth shine—
Moment by moment, O Lord, I am Thine.

Moment by moment I'm kept in His love,
Moment by moment I've life from above;
Looking to Jesus till glory doth shine,
Moment by moment, O Lord, I am Thine.

For Further Study

1. Why do many Christians *endure* the Christian life rather than *enjoy* it? Why is there often such barrenness in between the initial joy of finding forgiveness of sins and safe arrival in the halls of heaven? What is your life like in this regard?

2. In view of Galatians 2:20 and John 15:5, what is the outcome of trying to live the Christian life through human efforts rather than through depending on Christ? Do you sometimes try to live as a Christian in this way?

3. Jesus demonstrated total faith and dependence on the Father through the power of the Holy Spirit. What are the implications of this truth for your life?

Chapter One

Not I, But Christ

But when Peter had come to Antioch, I withstood him to his face, because he was to be blamed; for before certain men came from James, he would eat with the Gentiles; but when they came, he withdrew and separated himself, fearing those who were of the circumcision.

And the rest of the Jews also played the hypocrite with him, so that even Barnabas was carried away with their hypocrisy.

But when I saw that they were not straightforward about the truth of the gospel, I said to Peter before them all, "If you, being a Jew, live in the manner of Gentiles and not as the Jews, why do you compel Gentiles to live as Jews?

"We who are Jews by nature, and not sinners of the Gentiles, knowing that a man is not justified by the works of the law but by faith in Jesus Christ, even we have believed in Christ Jesus, that we might be justified by faith in Christ and not by the works of the law; for by the works of the law no flesh shall be justified.

"But if, while we seek to be justified by Christ, we ourselves also are found sinners, is Christ therefore a minister of sin? Certainly not!

"For if I build again those things which I destroyed, I make myself a transgressor.

"For I through the law died to the law that I might live to God.

"I have been crucified with Christ; it is no longer I who live, but Christ lives in me; and the life which I now live in the flesh I live by faith in the Son of God, who loved me and gave Himself for me.

"I do not set aside the grace of God; for if righteousness comes through the law, then Christ died in vain."

GALATIANS 2:11–21

Chapter One

Not I, But Christ

I have been crucified with Christ;
it is no longer I who live,
but Christ lives in me; and the life
which I now live in the flesh
I live by faith in the Son of God,
who loved me and gave Himself for me.

GALATIANS 2:20

I AM OFTEN ASKED TO SIGN MY NAME IN BIBLES OR BOOKS as I travel and minister the Word of God around the world. When I oblige, I usually append to my signature Galatians 2:20. This gives me an opportunity to tell people what this verse means and why it has become increasingly precious to me as the years have come and gone. Indeed, my testimony has now become the subject of this book!

Why is this verse so important to me? Because it gets to the heart of the most essential matters of the Christian life. As F. B. Meyer puts it, this is Paul's "confession of the power of the cross in his own life. It stood between him and the past. His self-life was nailed there, and this new life was no longer derived from vain efforts to keep the Law, but from the indwelling and [overflowing] of the life of Jesus—the perennial spring of John 4:14."[1]

Before we look at Galatians 2:20 in detail, however, we need to examine briefly the context, the content, and the challenge of this matchless verse.

The Context of This Verse. "When Peter had come to

Antioch, I withstood him to his face, because he was to be blamed" (Gal. 2:11). The whole background of the confrontation between Paul and Peter is beyond the purpose of this book. In fact, too many "unknowns" have boggled greater minds than mine. What is clear is that Paul "stood up" to Peter for a good reason. Peter was to be blamed. He was acting not only against his conscience but, more importantly, against the revelation he had received from God (see Acts 10 and 15).

What stirred Paul's holy indignation was the deceitfulness and compromise of Peter. In Antioch Peter had shared meals (including, perhaps, the Lord's Supper) with non-Jewish Christians. Everyone knew this and rejoiced. Peter was the first apostle to evangelize Gentiles (Acts 10, 11, 15) and was, therefore, to be trusted. But when "certain men came from James [the pastor of the Jerusalem church] . . . he withdrew [from this fellowship with Gentiles] . . . *fearing those who were of the circumcision* [Jews]" (2:12). This disorderly behavior seriously influenced "the rest of the Jews" [in the church] who "played the hypocrite with him"—including Barnabas who "was carried away with their hypocrisy" (Gal. 2:13).

This deceitfulness and compromise were more than playacting; they were, in fact, an adverse reflection on the gospel of the grace of God and the unity of the church of God. By his bad example, Peter was implying that Gentile believers who were saved by grace alone, through faith alone, needed to "live . . . as the Jews" (2:14), and that law-keeping and circumcision rituals were necessary for acceptance by God. This was, in essence, heresy!

Whatever else we can say about Peter, *he was dodging the message of the cross!* For as we shall see in a moment, to be justified by the grace of God is to die—as far as the law is concerned, so as to live—as far as God is concerned.

And this is not the first time Peter was rebuked for dodging the crucified life. It happened after his great confession at Caesarea Philippi. What could be clearer than his words "You are the Messiah, the Son of the living God"? So sound and fundamental was this declaration that Jesus said to him, "Blessed are you, Simon son of Jonah! For flesh and blood has not revealed this to you, but my Father in heaven. And I tell you, you are Peter, and on this rock I will build my church, and the gates of Hades will not prevail against it. I will give you the keys of the kingdom of heaven, and whatever you bind on earth will be bound in heaven, and whatever you loose on earth will be loosed in heaven."

Yet shortly afterward, when "Jesus began to show his disciples that he must go to Jerusalem, and undergo great suffering at the hands of the elders and chief priests and scribes, and be killed, and on the third day be raised," we read that "Peter took him aside and began to rebuke him, saying, 'God forbid it, Lord! This must never happen to you!'" But the Lord "turned and said to Peter, 'Get behind me, Satan! You are a stumbling block to me; for you are setting your mind not on divine things but on human things.'" Then the Master added: "'If any want to become my followers, let them deny themselves, and take up their cross and follow me. For those who want to save their life will lose it, and those who lose their life for my sake will find it. For what will it profit them if they gain the whole world but for-

feit their life? Or what will they give in return for their life?'"
(Matt. 16:13-26, NRSV).

Peter's refusal to accept the way of the cross eventually led
to the shameful denial of his Lord—even after boasting that he
would lay down his life for Jesus' sake (John 13:37; see Matt.
26:30-35; Mark 14:30-31; Luke 22:31-34). But that was before
Pentecost and, therefore, somewhat understandable.

But for you and me there is no excuse since we have the Holy
Spirit. And yet we are living in an hour when the message of the
"crucified life" is the last thing many professing Christians want
to hear. They adore the cradle of Christ and await the coming
of Christ, but they abhor the cross of Christ. For many religious
people, the cross is either a stumbling block or a laughing stock
(1 Cor. 1:23). For this reason the message of this book is so necessary for true overcomers in the Christian life.

The Content of This Verse. Paul spells this out in no uncertain terms: "A person is justified not by the works of the law but
through faith in Jesus Christ . . . that we might be justified by
faith in Christ, and not by doing the works of the law, because
no one will be justified by the works of the law. But if, in our effort
to be justified in Christ, we ourselves have been found to be sinners, is Christ then a servant of sin? Certainly not! But if I build
again the very things that I once tore down, then I demon-
strate that I am a transgressor. For through the law I died to the
law, so that I might live to God" (Gal. 2:16-19, NRSV). Here, in
substance, is the great doctrine of justification by grace through
faith. Martin Luther expounded on this passage:

This is the truth of the Gospel. It is also the principal article of all Christian doctrine, wherein the knowledge of all godliness consisteth. Most necessary it is, therefore, that we should know this article well, *teach it unto others, and beat it into their heads continually* [my emphasis].[2]

Read the preceding verses again and follow Paul's argument. Taking his text from Psalm 143:2, Paul interprets what he means by justification. The word *justified* occurs four times as a verb in verses 16 and 17 and once as a noun in verse 21. To summarize what Paul teaches in this passage I quote John R. W. Stott:

Jesus Christ came into the world to live and to die. In His life His obedience to the law was perfect. In His death He suffered for our disobedience. On earth He lived the only life of sinless obedience to the law which has ever been lived. On the cross He died for our law-breaking, since the penalty for disobedience to the law was death. All that is required of us to be justified, therefore, is to acknowledge our sin and helplessness, to repent of our years of self-assertion and self-righteousness, and to put our whole trust and confidence in Jesus Christ to save us.

"Faith in Jesus Christ," then, is not intellectual conviction only, but personal commitment. The expression in the middle of verse 16 is (literally) "we have believed *into (eis)* Christ Jesus." It is an act of committal, not just assenting to the fact that Jesus lived and died, but running to Him for refuge and calling on Him for mercy.[3]

So justification is not only a legal fact in which we are declared righteous by a holy God; it is also a transforming experience through a living identification with Christ (v. 17). By union with Christ we are radically transformed; we can no longer go back to our old life, for in Christ we are "a new creation" (2 Cor. 5:17).

This brings us to:

The Challenge of This Verse. "I have been crucified with Christ; it is no longer I who live, but Christ lives in me; and the life which I now live in the flesh I live by faith in the Son of God, who loved me and gave Himself for me" (Gal. 2:20). In this matchless statement Paul the apostle encapsulates the gospel of the grace of God. It is *the gospel of the extinguished life*—"I have been crucified with Christ" (Gal. 2:20). We have died to the law. By dying *with* Christ, who died under the law's penalty, we find that all the law's demands were satisfied in Him. They have no more hold on us. Being crucified, moreover, means that we have died to self. The dominating control of the fallen nature has been broken. If we do not understand this, then we are missing something very important. The extinguished life means death to self and sin.

In his book *The Christ-Life for the Self-Life* (addresses delivered mainly at Carnegie Hall, New York, during an ever-memorable week), F. B. Meyer writes:

> The curse of the Christian and of the world is that self is our pivot; it is because Satan made self his pivot that he became a devil. Take heaven from its center in God, and try to center it in self, and you transform heaven into hell. . . . The philos-

ophy of the Bible is to do away with self and to make Christ all in all. When dealing with a drunkard I am inclined to say to him, "Be a man." What a fool I am! I am trying to cast out the evil of drink by the evil of self-esteem. If I want to save a man, I must cast out the spirit of self and substitute the Lord Jesus Christ. Alpha, Omega, all in all. But how? . . . This epistle to the Galatians is my battle-axe. Luther used it for justification, but I think it is for sanctification [see Appendix B]. How? By the cross, and by the cross as presented in the epistle to the Galatians. [see 2:20; 3:1; 5:24; 6:14].

The apostle tells us in Galatians 1:4: "Jesus Christ . . . gave Himself for our sins, that He might deliver us from this present evil world, according to the will of God and our Father." He considers the cross in its aspect toward sanctification. He says: "He delivered us from this present evil world." In Romans we have the cross for justification; the putting away of sin; in Galatians for sanctification, the cross standing between me and my past, between me and the world, between me and myself.[4]

So in Galatians 2:20 we have the gospel of the extinguished life. But it is also *the gospel of the relinquished life*—"It is no longer I who live, but Christ lives in me" (Gal. 2:20). No longer is our life self-centered but Christ-centered. By the ministry of the Holy Spirit (as we shall see later) the Lord Jesus lives out His life in us day by day as we maintain total dependence on Him. The apostle says the same thing in his letter to the Romans, exhorting his readers to "present [themselves] to God as being alive from the dead and [their] members as instruments of righteousness to God" (Rom. 6:13). We do not relinquish ourselves to an enemy, but we present ourselves as a bride to the bridegroom who has wooed and won us in love.

As a pastor I have had the privilege of marrying couples times without number. As the two stand before me, I say to the bride, "Will you have this man to be your lawful wedded husband?" She answers in two words, "I will," and they are joined for life. That is the kind of presentation we are thinking of when we speak of the relinquished life. We are saying in effect, "Lord, I am married to You, being alive from the dead, to bring forth fruit unto God. Lord, from now on my language and life are two words: 'I will.'" Every day we must repeat that once-for-all interaction: "I am wholly Yours, Lord. Use me for Your glory."

Once again it is *the gospel of the distinguished life*—"The life which I now live in the flesh I live by faith in the Son of God, who loved me and gave Himself for me" (Gal. 2:20). That phrase, "faith in the Son of God," is loaded with rich meaning. Because of our union with Christ crucified and risen, we are "partakers of the divine nature" (2 Pet. 1:4); we actually share with the Son of God the distinguished life.

Two aspects of this distinctive life are spelled out for us. As the Son of God, our Lord in His perfect humanity chose to live a *dependent* life. He lived by faith (see John 5:19, 30; 6:57; 8:28; and 14:10). We also must live by faith (Rom. 1:17; Heb. 11:6). This life of dependence should be our distinctive. Anything less than this is to live in sin, "for whatever is not [of] faith is sin" (Rom. 14:23).

The other distinctive is that the Son of God lived a *devoted* life. He "gave Himself for [us]" (Gal. 2:20). That takes in the entire sweep of His life, service, and even death, in response to the will of His Father. In similar fashion, we are called to the high and holy distinction of yielding ourselves to God as living sacrifices so that we might "prove what is that good and acceptable and perfect will of God" (Rom. 12:1–2). Dependence on God and devotion to God are the marks of divine distinction. Such distinctiveness can be detected anywhere and under any circumstances by a watching world. Out of such a life the streams of living water flow in blessing to others.

Certainly this is the testimony of God's people throughout the centuries. Martin Luther experienced this blessing:

> He was a show-piece of discipline and penance, and self-denial and self-torture. "If ever," he said, "a man could be saved by monkery, that man was I." He had gone to Rome; it was considered to be an act of great merit to climb the Scala Sancta, the great sacred stairway, on hands and knees. He toiled upwards seeking that merit that he might win; and suddenly there came to him the voice from heaven: "The just shall live by faith." The life at peace with God was not to be attained by this futile, never-ending, ever-defeated effort; it could only be had by casting himself on the love and mercy of God as Jesus Christ has revealed them to men. It is when a man gives up the struggle which the pride of self thinks it can win, but must ever lose, and when he abandons himself to the forgiving love of God that peace must come.[5]

The blessing that flowed from Luther's life changed the face of Europe and, ultimately, the fate of millions. John Wesley was one of those affected. Here was a cultured mind, matched only by his spiritual sensitivity, servant attitude, and social concern. But he was a discouraged man as he returned to England from Savannah, Georgia. He had encountered great problems in his attempt to deal with the colonists in the New World. Indeed, these outward and inward battles brought him to doubt his own acceptability before the God he loved and served. In this frame of mind he went one evening—most reluctantly—to a meeting where Luther's *Preface to the Epistle to the Romans* was read. During the reading Wesley's "heart was strangely warmed." He recorded in his journal:

> I felt I did trust in Christ alone for salvation; and an assurance was given to me that He had taken away my sins, even mine, and saved me from "the law of sin and death."[6]

Armed with this message of union with Christ in His death and resurrection, John Wesley embarked on forty years of ministry that beggars description. So mightily did the Spirit of God use him that revivals blazed in England and America throughout the eighteenth and nineteenth centuries, and the course of history was changed.

In his book *They Found the Secret,*[7] the beloved former president and chancellor of Wheaton College, Dr. V. Raymond Edman, shares the testimonies of men and women who experienced the blessing of life "in Christ." His purpose "was to show . . . how the power of Christ, [which he called] 'the indwelling life of Christ,' was the source of every believer's spiritual strength." Feeling that evangelicals had largely neglected this theme for many years, Dr. Edman wanted to "put the idea into the mainstream of Christian thought so that all could benefit by entering into a life-transforming relationship with Christ. It is not enough just to know about Christ or to know about what He did for us or even to experience His work in us. What is needed is to experience *Him* in us as He works out God's inscrutable will."[8] Here are the testimonies of a few who discovered the secret of the exchanged life.

The crisis of the deeper life came to *John Bunyan* one day as he was walking in the fields. "Suddenly," he said, "this sentence fell upon my soul, *'Thy righteousness is in heaven.'* And me thought, with awe, I saw, with the eyes of my soul Jesus Christ at God's right hand. . . . It was glorious to me to see his exaltation and the worth and prevalency of all his benefits." . . . Ephesians 5:30 became "a sweet word" to him: "For we are members of his body, of his flesh, and of his bones." He could say: ". . . the Lord did also lead me into the mystery of union with the Son of God. . . . By this also was my faith in him, as my righteousness, the more confirmed in me; for if he and I were one, then his righteousness was mine, his merits mine, his victory also mine. Now I could see myself in heaven and earth at once; in heaven by my Christ, by my head, by my righteousness and life, though on earth by my body or person." . . .

And what were the results of Bunyan's being unchained from his doubts and fears? . . . Among them he lists *grace* that could keep him in deepest difficulties, *insight* into the Scriptures, *no fear* of death, an *assurance* of his Lord's presence with him, and a *fruitful service* for the Savior both in the pulpit and in the prison.[9]

———

September 18, 1884, marked the great crisis in the life of *Handley Moule*. Afterward he referred again and again to that date as a new departure in his life, a date when the reality and secret of a holy life became revealed to him.

The [Keswick] convention at Polmont was held in a great barn. . . . [Moule] sat in the audience in a critical state of mind, but also with "hunger for some gracious thing, if it was to be found." A Christian businessman, William Sloan, spoke from Haggai 1:6: "Ye eat, but ye have not enough." Self, he pointed out, is the source of leanness in the soul. Then Evan H. Hopkins spoke, emphasizing that man, even an earnest Christian, cannot live in victory by his own merit and efforts, but that what man cannot do, the Spirit of God could accomplish in him. Observed Moule: "He piled up the promises of God to the soul that will do two things towards Him: surrender itself into His hands and trust Him for His mighty victory within."

Just where he sat, Bishop Moule, the unsatisfied man of God, did two things: he yielded himself wholly and without reservation to the Savior as His bondslave, and he trusted definitely that the Lord Jesus would effect in him that transformation into His own image which the Lord alone can accomplish. . . .

In his able and analytical exposition of *The Spiritual Unfolding of Bishop H. C. G. Moule*, John Baird summarizes excellently the transformation that then transpired. . . . "He swung open the doors of his heart in his welcome to Jesus to be evermore his Lord. . . . He found comfort in the thought that he was now in the keeping of a gracious Redeemer. He

entered into abundance of blessing and fullness of life . . .
—not life merely endured, nor life as a task, nor life as a
struggle—but life as a joy and a victory with the spiritual
forces of the soul undivided.

The all-sufficiency of Jesus for sanctification was the vivifying truth. . . . He had felt holiness to be a vain endeavor in
his own strength. But Christian hope took on a new splendor.
A peace filled him like the calm falling on a troubled sea, as
he felt himself swept with willing mind into prompt and
exulting acceptance. . . . [His decision] was never regretted,
and it was never undone. Rather, it was repeated and recon-
firmed day by day. . . . The trust he reposed in Jesus had been
abundantly honored and satisfied. . . .

And what was the open secret of the saint in surplice? It
was simply this, he said, "Holiness by faith, a life humbly true
to God, made possible, made actual, by the use, for victory,
of the trusted Christ within."[10]

The pattern of *Charles G. Trumbull*'s experience is like that of
every other man of God who has come to know that "Christ
liveth in me, and the life which I now live in the flesh, I live
by the faith of the Son of God." . . . First, he was aware of
great fluctuations in his spiritual life. . . . Then there was the
matter of "failure before besetting sins." . . . Despite earnest
prayer for deliverance, abiding victory was not his experience. The third conscious lack was "in the matter of dynamic,
convincing spiritual power that would work miracle changes
in other men's lives." He was an active Christian, engaged in
many duties and responsibilities . . . even doing personal
work . . . *but . . . [he] wasn't seeing results.* . . .

The hunger of heart became more intense when he heard a preacher speak on Ephesians 4:12–13. . . . He was talking about Christ . . . in a way that . . . was utterly unknown to [him]. . . . "I expected him to give us a series of definite things that we could do to strengthen our Christian life . . . but his opening words showed me my mistake while they made my heart leap with a new joy. What he said was something like this: *'The resources of the Christian life, my friends, are just—Jesus Christ.'* That was all. But that was enough. . . ."

That summer he was attending a young people's missionary conference. . . . He heard again that the "rivers of living water" in a Christian's life should flow continuously and irresistibly, not intermittently. . . .

The next morning [Trumbull] prayed it out with God . . . And God . . . gave [him] . . . a new [experience of] Christ. . . . Wherein was the change? . . . "To begin with, I realized for the first time that the many references throughout the New Testament to Christ in you, you in Christ, Christ our life, and abiding in Christ are literal, actual, blessed fact, and not figures of speech. How the fifteenth chapter of John thrilled with new life as I read it now! And Ephesians 3:14–21. And Galatians 2:20. And Philippians 1:21."

No longer was Dr. Trumbull's faith only in the Christ who had died on the cross for our sins. His faith was now also in the Savior who dwells within the believer. "At last I realized," he declared, "that Jesus Christ was actually and literally within me; and even more than that, He had constituted Himself my very life, taking me into union with Himself— my body, mind, and spirit—while I still had my own identity and free will and full moral responsibility. . . . It meant that I need never again ask Him to help me as though He were one and I another, but rather simply to do His work, His will in me, and with me, and through me. . . . Jesus Christ had constituted Himself my life—not as a figure of speech . . . but as a literal, actual fact." . . .

Dr. Trumbull learned that the flow of that life was dependent on two simple conditions. After having received the Lord Jesus as personal Savior, there is *first* surrender, an absolute and unconditional surrender to the Savior as Lord and Master of one's life, irrespective of the cost; and *second*, the quiet act of faith, apart from any feeling or immediate evidence that God does set the trusting soul wholly free from the law of sin. . . .

"Jesus Christ does not want to be our helper; He wants to be our life. He does not want us to work for Him. He wants us to let Him do His work through us, using us as we use a pencil to write with—better still, using us as one of the fingers on His hand." . . . Dr. Trumbull was able *by that life* to lead many others into the life of victory.[11]

Devotional literature is replete with similar testimonies, but the few examples cited above illustrate the blessing we can *know* when we understand and *appropriate* the truth embodied in Galatians 2:20. As God's people, we must be willing to pray and mean:

> *Crucified with Christ, my Savior,*
> *I am dead to sin and shame;*
> *Now HIS LIFE rules my behavior—*
> *To the glory of His Name! Amen.*

Stephen F. Olford

For Further Study

1. In view of the context of Galatians 2:20, in what way was Peter dodging the message of the cross? In what ways do we? What are the results?

2. Why do Christian believers today—why do *we*—enjoy thinking and talking about Christ's birth and His future return, but sometimes shy away from considering His cross and its implications for daily life? Is the cross either a stumbling block or a laughing stock to you (see 1 Corinthians 1:23)? If so, why?

3. What is the core meaning of the biblical term *justification* (see Galatians 2:16-19)? What does it mean to you personally?

4. How do you feel about the author's statement that faith is not only intellectual conviction but personal commitment? Explain.

5. Is justification a legal pronouncement declaring us righteous before God, or a transforming experience, or both (see Galatians 2:17)? What does justification mean for your life today . . . tomorrow . . . in eternity?

6. What does the phrase "the exchanged life" mean to you? How do you feel about being crucified with Christ (dying to self) and about Jesus living His life through you (see Galatians 2:20)? What is your practical understanding of these key phrases?

Chapter Two

Not I, But Christ
and
His Death

What then are we to say? Should we continue in sin in order that grace may abound? By no means! How can we who died to sin go on living in it? Do you not know that all of us who have been baptized into Christ Jesus were baptized into his death? Therefore we have been buried with him by baptism into death, so that, just as Christ was raised from the dead by the glory of the Father, so we too might walk in newness of life.

For if we have been united with him in a death like his, we will certainly be united with him in a resurrection like his. We know that our old self was crucified with him so that the body of sin might be destroyed, and we might no longer be enslaved to sin. For whoever has died is freed from sin. But if we have died with Christ, we believe that we will also live with him. We know that Christ, being raised from the dead, will never die again; death no longer has dominion over him. The death he died, he died to sin, once for all; but the life he lives, he lives to God. So you also must consider yourselves dead to sin and alive to God in Christ Jesus.

Therefore, do not let sin exercise dominion in your mortal bodies, to make you obey their passions. No longer present your members to sin as instruments of wickedness, but present yourselves to God as those who have been brought from death to life, and present your members to God as instruments of righteousness. For sin will have no dominion over you, since you are not under law but under grace.

ROMANS 6:1–14, NRSV

Chapter Two

Not I, But Christ and His Death

I have been crucified with Christ.

GALATIANS 2:20

T HE NEW TESTAMENT CLEARLY TEACHES THAT THE battleground for all conflict in the Christian life takes place in the area that the Bible calls the "sinful flesh" (Rom. 8:3; Gal. 5:16–21). Whether the attack comes from the world or the devil, the offensive, ultimately, is fought right there. If we fail to appropriate what it means to be dead to sin but alive to God in Christ Jesus our Lord, then defeat in our Christian life is inevitable. We do well, then, to discover how we must die to our sinful flesh so that we will be able to affirm, "Not I, but Christ." This daily death involves three important considerations.

The Condemnation of Our Sinful Flesh

When Paul declares, "I have been crucified with Christ," he is interpreting the truth of Romans 8:3: "What the law could not do in that it was weak through the flesh, God did by sending His own Son in the likeness of sinful flesh. . . . He condemned sin in the flesh." The flesh could not be put to death without being condemned, so God sent His Son to accomplish this objective.

In the purpose of God this "condemnation" implied *the disclosure of the sinlessness of the Savior.* We are told that the Lord Jesus came in the *likeness* of sinful man ("man" is literally "flesh," Rom. 8:3) in order that He might condemn sin in the flesh. "The word *likeness* is important, for it signifies that Christ came in flesh like ours and was *true* Man, but not *sinful* Man. . . . He was free from sin both in nature and act."[1] This means that in His human body He so exhibited the holy life of absolute sinlessness that sinful flesh was condemned in every respect. His sinlessness emanated now and again in resplendent glory during His ministry, as on the Mount of Transfiguration.

I am reminded of the occasion when Jesus commanded Peter to let down the net on the right side of the boat—after a night of futile fishing. Peter, recognizing his Lord, obeyed; but when he returned to shore with a haul of fish, he caught a glimpse of Christ's resplendent holiness, the likes of which he had never seen before. The pure light of the Savior's sinlessness condemned sin in the flesh. Kneeling at Jesus' feet, he exclaimed, "Depart from me, for I am a sinful man, O Lord!" (Luke 5:8). John the apostle wrote of this searching sinlessness: "This is the condemnation, that . . . *light* has come into the world, and men loved darkness rather than light" (John 3:19). Jesus later reminded His disciples, "If I had not come . . . [people] would have no sin, but now they have no excuse for their sin" (John 15:22).

Have you ever been ushered into a brilliantly lighted room wearing dirty clothes? I recall this happening to me many years ago in Pennsylvania where I was invited to speak at a formal banquet. The plan was for me to arrive by train, check into my hotel, change my clothes, and have time to prepare before speaking at this auspicious event. Those were the days before air-conditioning, and trains were begrimed with smoke and soot. To make matters worse, there was no water with which to wash and freshen up, and the train was behind schedule. Eventually I arrived, and the excited—but exasperated—people who met me at the station took me directly to the banquet hall where folk were waiting to hear the young Englishman billed to bring the message. Everything looked beautiful—except me! I felt like a chimney sweep!

If this can be true of one physically defiled, what about the moral defilement of those who stand before the blazing light of Christ's holiness? In our corrupt world we can be filthy and not really know it until we "stand in the presence of Jesus the Nazarene." No wonder Paul declared, "All have sinned and [are falling] short of the glory of God" (Rom. 3:23). God has condemned our sinful flesh by the testing standard of His beloved Son. Therefore, the moment we measure ourselves by His holiness, we sense our own sinfulness.

But God not only condemned sinful flesh by the disclosure of the sinlessness of the Savior, but also by *the exposure of the sinfulness of the sinner*—"This is the condemnation," writes John, "that . . . men loved darkness rather than light, because their deeds were evil. For everyone practicing evil hates the light and does not come to the light, lest his deeds should be exposed" (John 3:19–20).

Paul had impeccable credentials. He could call himself "blameless" (Phil. 3:6); but then one day the Holy Spirit turned the searchlight of the Savior upon the sinfulness of his heart, and he had to confess, "For I would not have known covetous-ness unless the law had said, 'You shall not covet.' But sin, tak-ing opportunity by the commandment, produced in me all manner of evil desire. For apart from the law sin was dead. I was alive once without the law, but when the commandment came, sin revived and I died. And the commandment, which was to bring life, I found to bring death. For sin, taking occasion by the commandment, deceived me, and by it killed me. Therefore the law is holy, and the commandment holy and just and good"; and again: "For I know that in me (that is, in my flesh) nothing good dwells; for to will is present with me, but how to perform what is good I do not find. For the good that I will to do, I do not . . . but the evil I will not . . . do, that I practice."

Then he concludes with that shattering condemnation: "Now . . . it is no longer I who do it, but sin that dwells in me. . . . O wretched man that I am! Who will deliver me from this body of death? I thank God—through Jesus Christ our Lord! So then, with the mind I myself serve the law of God, but with the flesh the law of sin" (Rom. 7:7-12, 18-20, 24-25).

As F. F. Bruce puts it, "Some commentators have tried to illu-minate Paul's words by reference to Virgil's account of the Etruscan king Mezentius who tied his living captives to decom-posing corpses (*Aeneid,* viii. 485ff.). But Paul is not thinking of the body of flesh and blood; the evil was more deeply rooted. 'The body of this death,' or 'this body of death' (RSV), is, like the 'body of sin' (vi. 6), that heritage of human nature subject to the law of sin and death which he shares with all sons of Adam, that *massa perditionis* in which the whole of the old creation is involved, and from which, for all his longing and struggling, he cannot extricate himself by his own endeavors."[2]

Are we prepared to accept God's condemnation of our sinful flesh? To hesitate in our answer is to reveal that we have neither considered the sinlessness of the Savior or the sinfulness of our hearts. We must be prepared to accept the diagnosis of the divine Physician in order to experience the cure of victory.

The Crucifixion of Our Sinful Flesh

"I have been crucified with Christ" (Gal. 2:20). These words mean that our old self was crucified with Christ "so that the body of sin might be rendered powerless, that we should no longer be slaves to sin—because anyone who has died has been freed from sin" (Rom. 6:6-7, NIV). Observe that *this crucifixion with Christ is a past event.* We "*have been* crucified with Christ" (Gal. 2:20). The verb is in the perfect tense, indicating a completed action. This teaches us that the judicial (or positional) crucifixion of our sinful flesh took place some two thousand years ago—which is more easily understood when we remember that God judges the human race through one of two representatives: Adam or Christ. When Adam sinned, the human race sinned in him; when Jesus Christ came to redeem sinful people by His death, the human race died in Him. In Colossians 3:3 Paul writes, "you died" (past tense), denoting that our death dates from the death of Christ. The apostle goes on to tell us that when Christ died, "*He died to sin once*" (Rom. 6:10). This is something more than His death *for sins* (plural).

49

The penalty of our sins was fully dealt with by our Lord Jesus Christ, as was the power of *sin*.

Because we are united with Christ in His death, we share in the release from the dominion of sin. We are no longer under law, but under grace (Rom. 6:14). To the glory of God, all the objectives and ends of Christ's crucifixion were accomplished judicially in us! God's law can make no claim on our sinful flesh that has not been dealt with in Jesus Christ—because of our union with Him in His death.

Perhaps an illustration will help. Capt. Reginald Wallis wrote many books on the victorious life and made a tremendous impact on my life. He tells of an incident during the American Civil War when men were drawn by lot to join the army. A man named Wyatt was called up to fight for the South. He was the sole breadwinner for his very large family. Realizing this hardship, another young man named Pratt volunteered to go instead. He was accepted and drafted to the front, *bearing the name and number of Wyatt*.

Eventually Pratt was killed in battle, and having died as the substitute and in the name of the other man, the full name of Wyatt was recorded as killed in action. At a later date Wyatt was again called up for service, but at the recruiting office he calmly stated that *he had died already*. When the entry was researched, it was discovered that although the real Wyatt was alive and well, he was *dead in the eyes of the authorities* because he was identified with his substitute. Therefore, he went free.[3]

In the same way, when Jesus died, I died and, therefore, I am free. That is my positional status in the Lord Jesus Christ. As a result, God isn't going to expect my death since His Son was my substitute. This is the liberating truth of *identification* with Christ.

> *I'm dead to sin through Christ my Lord,*
> *For in His death I also died;*
> *It's written clear in God's own Word,*
> *And, praise His name, I'm justified!*
>
> *I'm dead to sin, thus I must live,*
> *To Christ alone who gave His all;*
> *And for His love I can't but give*
> *My life and gifts, both great and small.*
>
> *I'm dead to sin, so I must serve*
> *My God and King each day and hour;*
> *What He commands I must observe,*
> *And seek to do with heav'nly pow'r.*
>
> *I'm dead to sin, O blessed thought!*
> *I now can rest from care and strife;*
> *My fight He has forever fought,*
> *And now I live His risen life.*
>
> Stephen F. Olford

But, in the second place, *crucifixion with Christ is a present experience*—"I am crucified with Christ" (Gal. 2:20, KJV). While the verb is in the perfect passive indicative, the past action has spiritual benefits that are present realities, as the eminent Greek scholar Kenneth S. Wuest points out.[4] No doubt this is why the translators of the King James Version render the sentence as "I *am* crucified with Christ." The apostle includes the same idea when he exhorts believers in Rome to apply, by the power of the Spirit, the present realities of the cross to the "deeds of the body." He says, "If you are living according to the flesh, you must die; but if by the Spirit you are putting to death the deeds of the body, you will live" (Rom. 8:13, NASB). Here the verb is the present indicative. As we shall see, dying daily is a Calvary experience today. Jesus said, "If anyone desires to come after Me, let him deny himself, and *take up his cross DAILY, and follow Me*"(Luke 9:23). This is where the doctrine of the crucified life cuts deep into our hearts. That message is being preached little today. Taking up the cross represents willingness to accept all that the death of Christ denotes and demands in the present tense. We cannot crucify ourselves, *but we must be willing to be crucified.*

This present-tense crucifixion spells out three things that sophisticated cultural Christianity does not want to hear. But I repeat, the Master said, "If anyone desires to come after Me, let Him deny himself, and take up his cross daily, and follow Me" (Luke 9:23). We take up the cross in all its reality when we are willing to accept (1) *the cross of shame.* For the Lord Jesus, the cross meant shame. It is recorded that He "endured the cross, despising the *shame*" (Heb. 12:2). Therefore, by daily identification with our Lord Jesus Christ, the cross will mean *shame.*

Have you ever wondered why Moses fashioned a bronze serpent in the wilderness and set it on a pole (Num. 21:8–9)? It symbolized the deadly snakes that were stinging the children of Israel. In a far deeper sense, that bronze serpent foreshad-

owed the "body of sin" with which our Lord Jesus Christ identified Himself when He hung on the cross (John 3:14-15). Thus
Paul reminds us that He "who knew no sin" was made "to be sin
for us, that we might become the righteousness of God in Him"
(2 Cor. 5:21). And again, Galatians 3:13: "Christ has redeemed
us from the *curse* of the law, having become a curse for us (for it
is written, 'Cursed is everyone who hangs on a tree')." This is
both a mystery and a victory! Paul gloried in the cross because
he could no longer glory in the flesh (Gal. 6:14). The cross rep-
resented all that his sinful flesh deserved. As the hymnist put it:

> *I take, O cross, thy shadow for my abiding place—*
> *I ask no other sunshine than the sunshine of His face;*
> *Content to let the world go by, To know no gain nor loss,*
> *My sinful self my only shame, My glory all the cross.*

Elizabeth Clephane

Thus to accept the cross of shame is to "have no confidence in
the flesh" (Phil. 3:3). This is the evidence of *true reliance* in the
Christian life.

Present crucifixion with Christ not only means identifying
myself daily with the cross of shame, but also with (2) *the cross of
suffering*. The cross, for the Lord Jesus, involved "the suffering
of death" (Heb. 2:9), and it will mean the same for us (Phil. 1:29;
3:10). Some evidence suggests that when the Romans crucified
a man, the execution was recorded the moment the victim
was nailed to the cross—even though the individual might
linger for hours or even days.

In the same way, we are legally or judicially declared dead the moment we identify ourselves by saving faith with our Savior and Lord. However, as most of us know only too well, the flesh emerges again and again from the death of reckoning faith. Martin Luther put it well when he lamented, "The 'old man' dies hard." Those who hold that there is no conflict within the Christian because of the supposition that the old nature has been eradicated have a twofold problem. The first is biblical. They ignore such passages as Romans 7:13–25 and Galatians 5:13–16. The second is experiential. While the flesh is to become increasingly subdued as the Christian learns by grace to walk in the Spirit, the flesh is never eliminated. The child of God is never released from the necessity of consciously choosing to depend on divine grace.[5] Though present crucifixion is a painful experience, we must not relent.

> *It is the way the Master went;*
> *Should not the servant tread it still?*
>
> Horatius Bonar

Our natural tendency is to shrink from death and climb down from the cross. Our old nature wants to fight for our selfish rights and our selfish reputation, but self belongs on the cross. And suffering for Christ should function as nails to hold us to the cross that the life of Jesus might shine through our human personalities.

The saintly William Law said, "Take every such occasion with both hands as a blessed occasion of dying to self" (*The*

Keswick Week, 1948). A missionary on furlough once shared the following testimony: "The greatest lesson I've learned this term is how to accept the nails that hold me to the cross." She explained, "There was a lady missionary with whom I lived and worked who adversely affected me from the very first day I met her. She had a frame of mind, a way of speaking, which utterly distressed me; and the longer we lived together, the more I wondered whether I would even maintain my sanity. After struggling in prayer about the matter, God taught me the meaning of 'taking up my cross.' From then on I regarded that lady as the nails that kept me to the cross. The more I accepted those nails, the more I loved her, and the more peace and joy flooded my soul." She concluded by saying, "I have already told our Field Director that I want to spend my next term alongside that same lady, for I wouldn't have missed the blessing for anything."[6]

So often we talk about being hurt. Perhaps someone has wounded or grieved us. But it is usually the uncrucified flesh that resents the hurt, and it should die! We need to learn to "accept the nails" that hold us to the cross so that the Christ-life is magnified through our mortal bodies. To accept the cross of suffering, in union with Christ, is to learn obedience by the things we suffer (see Heb. 5:8). This is the evidence of true *obedience* in the Christian life.

Leonard Ravenhill aptly described the Apostle Paul as a man who "had no ambitions [for himself]—and so had nothing to be jealous about. He had no reputation—and so had nothing to fight about. He had no possessions—and therefore nothing to worry about. He had no 'rights'—so therefore he could not suffer wrong. He was already broken—so no one could break him. He was 'dead'—so none could kill him. He was less than the least—so who could humble him? He had suffered the loss of all things—so none could defraud him."[7]

But present identification with Christ not only means bearing the cross of shame and suffering but, even more deeply, it involves willingness to accept daily (3) *the cross of sacrifice.* It is written that "for the joy that was set before Him [Jesus] *endured the cross*, despising the shame" (Heb. 12:2). In Philippians 2:8 we read that He was "obedient to the point of death, even the death of the cross." Dietrich Bonhoeffer wrote, "When Christ calls a man, He bids him come and die."[8] How many of us are prepared to die to our reputation, to our rights, to our riches—indeed, to everything but Jesus? This is why we are exhorted in Hebrews 12 to "consider Him who endured such hostility from sinners against Himself, lest [we] become weary and discouraged in [our] souls." Our task is to resist to the point of "bloodshed, striving against sin" (Heb. 12:3, 4). This is the evidence of true *endurance* in the Christian life. We are tempted to conform to the world, and the great cry from our contemporaries is to "get with it." We need to heed Christ's call to "go forth to Him, *outside* the camp, bearing His reproach" (Heb. 13:13). Paul states it magnificently when he declares, "God forbid that I should glory except in the cross of our Lord Jesus Christ, by whom the world has been crucified to me, and I to the world" (Gal. 6:14). This means walking the Calvary road, even unto death.

Are we prepared to accept the past and present implications of crucifixion with Christ? It is one thing to say, "I have been crucified with Christ" (Gal. 2:20), but it is quite another matter to ". . . take up His cross daily, and follow [Him]" (Luke 9:23).

But there's a third—and very important—point that we must yet ponder.

The Cancellation of the Sinful Flesh

When we affirm "I have been crucified with Christ" (Gal. 2:20), we should be able to sing with Charles Wesley:

> *He breaks the power of canceled sin,*
> *He sets the prisoner free.*

Paul informs us that the one who has died with Christ "has been freed from sin" (Rom. 6:7, NIV). If our old self is condemned and crucified, then we can venture out on the sound assumption that the "body of sin" is done away with, rendered powerless, inoperative, put out of business (Rom. 6:6). To make this cancellation of the sinful flesh good in personal experience demands a twofold discipline.

First, *we must reckon on the past FACT of our oneness with Christ in death to the sinful flesh*—"What shall we say then? Shall we continue in sin that grace may abound? Certainly not! How shall we who died to sin live any longer in it? . . . Do you not know that as many of us as were baptized into Christ Jesus were baptized into His death?" (Rom. 6:1–3). The apostle questions, "Why are you so ignorant about the grace of God? Why are you hankering after antinomianism, saying, 'The more we sin, the more the grace of God abounds'?" We must reckon on the fact that we have died to our sinful self (see Appendix C).

Our identification with Christ is a *fact*, and the relevant words are "Likewise . . . reckon yourselves to be dead indeed to sin. . . . Do not let sin reign in your mortal body, that you should obey it in its lusts. . . . Do not present your members as instruments of unrighteousness to sin" (Rom. 6:11–13).

To count on our oneness with Christ in death to the sinful flesh is to proceed on the definite assumption that we are dead to every call and claim of sin. In the light of all that sovereign grace has done, we must repudiate every attempt of sin to seduce and master us. Our language must be just as bold as the apostle's when he asks, "Shall we continue in sin that grace may abound?" and then exclaims, "Certainly not! How shall we who died to sin live any longer in it?" (Rom. 6:1–2). When sin knocks at the door of our lives, we should refuse, by the power of the Holy Spirit, to let it enter. Not to do so is to show that we have never understood the meaning of God's redeeming work in Christ.

Augustine knew what Paul was talking about. Early in his Christian life one of his former sinful companions, a prostitute, encountered him on the street with a smile and said, "Augustine, it is I."

He looked at her and replied, "But it is not I," and turned away.[9]

Augustine acted on the fact that he was dead to his sinful flesh; consequently, he would not allow sin to reign in his mortal body, nor would he yield his members as "instruments of unrighteousness to sin" (Rom. 6:13). We, too, must reckon on the cancellation of our sinful flesh and refuse to "make . . . provision for the flesh, to fulfill its lusts" (Rom. 13:14). That is a powerful verse—the verse that changed Augustine's life.

I knew an outstanding Christian layman, A. Lindsay Glegg, after whom my son David is named. He lectured us in seminary on the art of sermon illustration. He had twin sons. One became a brilliant engineer who designed and built fast racing cars that won many races. The other was a commercial artist whom Sir Winston Churchill commissioned to produce camouflage covering for the industrial areas of London during World War II. When they were just boys, the two of them went for a ride on their bicycles. Knowing they would pass the "old swimming hole," their father warned, "You may ride your bikes, but don't you dare swim today."

Off they went! Eventually they returned looking jolly but perhaps a little jittery as well. Lindsay Glegg inspected the rear of one of the bicycles and, sure enough, detected a trickle of water. He opened the canvas bag strapped to the seat and found two wet swimming trunks in it. Calling his two sons, he asked, "Didn't I tell you not to swim?"

"Yes, Dad," they replied in unison.

"Well, why did you take your swimming trunks along?"

Their answer was classic: "Just in case we might be tempted!"

Paul commands: "Make [present imperative] no provision for the flesh, to fulfill its lusts" (Rom. 13:14). For example, if you know that pornographic literature will make you renounce the cross of shame, suffering, and sacrifice, then tear it up and burn it! "Flee . . . youthful lusts" (2 Tim. 2:22). There is such a thing as *strategic withdrawal* in the battle of life.

But not only must we reckon on the past *fact* of our oneness with Christ, but *we must rely on the present FORCE of our oneness with Christ in death to the sinful flesh.* Paul says, "If you live according to the flesh you will die; but if *by the Spirit* you [go on putting] to death the deeds of the body, *you will live*" (Rom. 8:13). This is both simple and *powerful!* It affirms that whenever we deliberately count on our *union* with Christ in His death, the Holy Spirit instantly applies the crucifying force of the cross to the ever-reviving flesh, thus making the life of victory a reality in our experience (see Appendix D).

When Jesus hung on Calvary's cross, the moment came when He consciously and firmly positioned His head and prayed, "'Father, into Your hands I commend My spirit'" (Luke 23:46). But during the process of crucifixion He yielded Himself "in *weakness* . . . through the eternal Spirit" (2 Cor. 13:4; Heb. 9:14). During His lifetime evil men tried to throw Him over the hilltop (Luke 4:29). Others attempted to stone Him (John 8:59), but He knew there was only one way He would die, and that was by total submission to crucifixion (Luke 22:42). He gave Himself in the weakness of nonresistance to be nailed to those wooden beams so that that cross might ever be both the *message* of salvation and the *method* of salvation.

You may ask, "What do you mean by the method of salvation?" The answer is that the cross is never self-inflicted. We don't retreat to a monastery of self-flagellation. We submit ourselves to the Holy Spirit who alone can take the crucifying power of the cross and apply it to rising sinful self every time it rears its ugly head (Rom. 8:13). If we're tempted to be ill-tempered with our wives or our children or to become mean-spirited with some deacon or church member, we trust the Holy Spirit to "put to death the deeds of the body" (Rom. 8:13). Then the sweetness and love of the Lord Jesus come through instead. That's the message and method of victorious living!

So be kind at the breakfast table when you're not feeling up to par and you're tempted to snap at everyone. From experience I know that within each of us God has built what I call a spiritual radar system. When self is tempted to rise, conscience sends a warning signal so that there is time to lift up a prayer to heaven. Thus, instead of being caustic, you look at your spouse and say, "Sweetheart, I love you." As you sip your coffee, your son may be acting up. You have a choice. You can speak to him in "tough love" or provoke him to anger. As self rises on such occasions, nail it to the cross by the power of the Spirit. Share something with your boy that will make him look into your face and say, "Dad (or Mom), I love you." That's what the Christ-life is all about.

Harold St. John was greatly beloved among the Christian Brethren of England. He knew Hebrew and Greek and expounded God's Word in great power and richness. Indeed, he gave me more insights into this life of victory than I will ever be able to recall. One story he told went something like this.

In South America many years ago, an engineering firm was commissioned to work on a big project. Ultimately the task had to be abandoned because so many died of malaria. But before the work force was totally disbanded, the thickly wooded land was set afire in order to cleanse the infected area. About two years later the workmen returned to resume operations and were surprised to find the blackened ground covered with a new and unknown type of plant with an exquisite blue flower. Specimens were gathered and forwarded to botanical gardens around the world, but no one could identify the bloom that had resulted from the fire.

What a parable this is of sinful flesh that has received the Spirit's application of the mortifying force of the cross! From the sentence of death to our sinful flesh can spring up the blue flower of victory in Jesus!

In a lovely spot in England there's a church called St. Alban's Abbey. Walking through that abbey one day, I saw these words and jotted them down.

> *I hung upon the cross for thee,*
> *Cease from sinning now for Me;*
> *CEASE—I pardon,*
> *FIGHT—I help,*
> *CONQUER—I crown.*

This is victory. Hallelujah!

For Further Study

1. What does Christ's sinlessness have to do with our sinfulness (see Romans 8:3; John 3:19-20)? How does His perfection condemn sin in us? Is devout religion the cure for sin? Why or why not?

2. How is our crucifixion with Christ both a past event and a present reality (Romans 6:6-7)? What did the Apostle Paul really mean by "crucified with Christ"? What does this phrase mean to you?

3. In what sense are we not under law but under grace (see Romans 6:14)? Define each term in your own words; then support the definitions with several Scriptures. How would you explain to someone else that Christ's death has fulfilled the law in us?

4. What does it mean for a Christian today to take up Christ's cross (Luke 9:23)? Specifically, what does this mean for your life? In what ways does this bring you shame, suffering, and sacrifice?

5. Do you agree that it is usually the uncrucified flesh that resents the hurts in our lives? Are we actually meant to die to such hurts (see Hebrews 5:8)? Is this happening in your life?

6. Romans 6 says that our old self has been rendered powerless; Romans 13 tells us to "make no provision for the flesh." What is the interrelationship between what Christ has accomplished and the choices we make day by day? How is this playing out in your life?

Chapter Three

Not I, But Christ
and
His Life

For this reason I bow my knees to the Father of our Lord Jesus Christ, from whom the whole family in heaven and earth is named, that He would grant you, according to the riches of His glory, to be strengthened with might through His Spirit in the inner man, that Christ may dwell in your hearts through faith; that you, being rooted and grounded in love, may be able to comprehend with all the saints what is the width and length and depth and height—to know the love of Christ which passes knowledge; that you may be filled with all the fullness of God.

Now to Him who is able to do exceedingly abundantly above all that we ask or think, according to the power that works in us.

EPHESIANS 3:14–20

Chapter Three

Not I, But Christ and His Life

It is no longer I who live, but Christ lives in me.

GALATIANS 2:20

IN OUR LAST CHAPTER WE FOCUSED ON DEATH TO OUR sinful flesh as the Holy Spirit keeps our old self nailed to the cross (Roman 6; 8:13). We learned that if we live according to the *flesh*, everything we do will wither and die. But if by the *Spirit* we go on mortifying (putting to death) the deeds of the body (here "body" is equivalent to "the flesh" as in Romans 6:6),[1] we shall live to the glory of God.

In this chapter I want to examine the vivifying truth of Christ as our life (Col. 3:4). By nature we are "dead in trespasses and sins" (Eph. 2:1). But when Christ becomes alive to us and in us, all that changes. Paul experienced this resurrection life in Christ, and he could testify, "It is no longer I who live, but Christ lives in me" (Gal. 2:20). Of course, this happened initially at his conversion on that Damascus road (Acts 9).

But to say and mean "Christ lives in me" is more than conversion. Many theologians call it progressive sanctification. Three aspects of this truth suggest themselves:

The Miracle of Christ's Indwelling

"Christ lives in me" (Gal. 2:20). These words mean more than Christ's initial entrance. I am assuming that this has happened to you already. I am accepting the fact that you and I have bowed at the cross; we have experienced redemption through the precious blood; we have been regenerated by the Holy Spirit; we have been baptized into the body of Christ. As a result Christ is alive in us by His indwelling Spirit (Rom. 6:3–4).

This is one of the greatest miracles and mysteries of Holy Scripture. In describing this to the church at Colossae, the apostle searched for words to convey the mystery hidden from humans and angels in all ages but now revealed to us, namely, "*Christ in you*, the hope of glory" (Col. 1:27). Paul proceeds to teach the Ephesian believers that this "mystery" takes place through *a miraculous operation*. He prays, "I bow my knees to the Father . . . that He would grant you, according to the riches of His glory, to be strengthened with might through His Spirit in the inner man, that Christ may dwell in your hearts through faith" (Eph 3:14–17). In praying for this miraculous operation to take place, he has believers in mind—those who were already "sealed with the Holy Spirit of promise" (Eph. 1:13).

Dr. Handley Moule comments on this verse:

> Why do we need a supreme *empowering* just in order to receive [the Indweller]? Does the hungry wanderer need power in order to eat the food without which he will soon sink? Does the bewildered mariner need power to welcome onto his deck the pilot who alone can steer him to the haven of his desire? No; but there is another aspect of the matter here. For the heart, though it immeasurably needs the blessed Indweller, has that in it which *dreads His absolute indwelling* [italics mine]. . . . So the hand stretched out to "open the door" (Rev. 3:20) . . . falls again and shrinks from that turn-

ing of the key which is to set the last recess . . . open to the Master. Here is the need for the Spirit's empowering work.[2]

You may be wondering why so many Christians aren't rejoicing in the wonder of an indwelling Christ. They are afraid to make Jesus absolute Lord. They hesitate to throw open every door of the house life in which they dwell. Yes, He can come through the front door and go into the living room. He can go into the dining room and kitchen, but there are other rooms of the house they don't want Him to enter. So they keep those doors locked—the doors to those last inner recesses of the human personality. They don't want Him to be at home in their hearts. This is why they need the miraculous operation of the Holy Spirit in their lives.

Not only is a miraculous operation needed, but also *a miraculous revelation*. Paul had two encounters with our Lord Jesus Christ that especially impact our present study. First, on the road to Damascus God broke in on his soul and revealed Christ *to* him. By the illumination and enabling of the Holy Spirit he cried, "*Lord,* what do You want me to do?" (Acts 9:6). I believe his conversion took place right there, for "no one can say that Jesus is Lord except by the Holy Spirit" (1 Cor. 12:3). The second encounter occurred later when Christ was not only revealed *to* him, but Christ was also revealed *in* him. Galatians 1:15–16 states, "It pleased God, who . . . called me through His grace, to reveal His Son in me, that I might preach Him among the Gentiles."

Martin Luther offers us this beautiful insight:

Paul is saying, "When I was not yet born, God ordained me to be an apostle and in due time confirmed my apostleship before the world. Every gift, be it small or great, spiritual or temporal, and every good thing I should ever do, God has ordained while I was yet in my mother's womb where I could neither think nor perform any good thing. After I was born God supported me. Heaping mercy upon mercy, He freely forgave my sins, replenishing me with His grace to enable me to learn *what great things are ours in Christ* [italics mine]. To crown it all, He called me to preach the Gospel to others. . . . What prompted Him to call me? His grace alone."[3]

He had a revelation not only *of* Christ, but of great things *in* Christ. Christ was not only real to Him, but Christ was real in Him.

I remember the testimony of a missionary home on furlough. She had been overseas for a number of years without any real joy, spiritual power, or fruitfulness. She had gone to the mission field more from a desire to put her nursing skills into practice than from a compelling love for Christ and souls. Soon she became dissatisfied with the monotony of service and the barrenness of her own life. With spiritual hunger in her heart, she went to a spiritual life conference where she heard the message of the indwelling life of Christ. At the end of the service she asked the speaker for a private talk. She recounted how she had come to the field with great enthusiasm, but the whole experience had become so fruitless and frustrating that she was on the verge of going home.

As they sat down together, the preacher asked her, "Has

there ever been a time in your life when you asked Christ to come into your life, when you realized you were a sinner—'dead in trespasses and sins'? Are you aware that Christ died for your sins and shed His precious blood for the cleansing of your sins—that He rose again to be your living Savior and wants to come into your life? And have you asked Him in?"

She replied, "Yes, I have."

Then, pressing the matter further, God's servant posed this question: "Can you say, 'Christ lives in me *now*'?"

"No," she replied.

"Do this," counseled the man of God. "Go into a quiet room and recall that it was a miracle for Christ to come into your life in the first place. That was the miracle of regeneration. Now ask for the miracle of revelation. Verbalize this prayer: 'O God, reveal Your Son in me.'" (For some people these two miracles take place *consciously at the same time*.)

"It was all so simple," she explained, referring to the speaker's counsel. "At first I was disappointed. I thought he was going to give me some theological explanation and then tell me why I felt so frustrated and why I wanted to leave the field. But all he said was to ask God to reveal His Son in me." She went and knelt by her bedside, opened the Bible to that passage in Galatians 1:15–16, and prayed, "O God, reveal Your Son *in* me." Suddenly, the glory of that wonderful fact became a reality, and she burst into tears, and then into laughter and joy. Afterwards she went back and told the speaker, "I can't wait to go back to my work because Christ NOW is *alive in me!*"

I lived for many years as a Christian and even led people to

Jesus Christ before that truth broke in upon my life and changed me forever. Major Ian Thomas, author of *The Saving Life of Christ*, helped me. He had been studying to become a doctor. He was right at the top of his class and had won all kinds of awards, but then he learned that God expects nothing more or less from our self-life than utter failure (John 15:5). By studying the Word he further realized that God has condemned, crucified, and buried our sinful flesh and that Christ can be a living reality when He is revealed in us. This discovery was so transforming that Thomas dropped his studies and went into the ministry to share this Good News. Ever since, he has crisscrossed the world with the victorious message of the indwelling life of Christ. Do you know that experience in your life?

But I want to move on and emphasize that the miracle of Christ's indwelling must be followed by:

The Measure of Christ's Indwelling

The phrase "Christ lives in me" (Gal. 2:20) reminds me of that verse we so often use to lead sinners to Christ—Revelation 3:20. Actually, it's a message to the church and to the Christian within the church: "Listen! I am standing at the door and knocking; if you hear my voice and open the door, I will come in to you and eat with you, and you with me" (Rev. 3:20, NRSV). The Lord Jesus is standing outside of a constituted church where He has been dethroned from His place of sovereign authority. As a result, the church has become lukewarm; it is "neither cold nor hot." Because it is lukewarm, He warns of judgment. The church dares to assert, "[We are] rich . . . and . . . need nothing," and does not recognize that it is "wretched, pitiable, poor, blind, and naked." So the Lord counsels these lukewarm Christians to buy from Him gold refined in the fire—to restore a standard of value—and white garments to clothe the shame of nakedness and eye salve to cure spiritual blindness. "Repent," He commands as He stands and knocks at the door of the church that has ousted Him, and He asks to enter in all His fullness (Rev. 3:16–20). You ask, "What does that mean?" The simple answer is that He longs to indwell the individual believer and the church body as undisputed HOST.

Christ is already Guest in our lives. "I will . . . eat *with you*" (Rev. 3:20, NRSV). All genuine Christians know the indwelling Christ in that measure; otherwise they are not saved. Romans 8:9 declares that anyone who does not have the Spirit of Christ does not belong to Him. But Christ can dwell in our lives as Guest—and only as Guest! The majority of Christians, who are neither effective in their churches or in the world in which they live, have this problem. They are converted but carnal. They are out of Egypt but have never entered Canaan. They claim to be committed to the Word, but they are conformed to the world (Rom. 12:2). Christ lives in their hearts, but He is only a Guest.

The text, however, teaches a deeper truth: *Christ must be altogether Host in our lives.* "If you . . . open the door, I will come in to you and eat with you, and *you with me*" (Rev. 3:20 NRSV). That insight transformed the ministry of Dr. F. B. Meyer, one of the great preachers of a past generation (1847–1929). In philanthropic and political matters, he could fill the largest churches and halls in the British Isles and hold people spellbound with his utterances. But he had no message of life—none whatsoever! Dr. J. C. Pollock sums it up this way:

> In his first independent charge at York, Meyer "didn't know anything about conversion or about the gathering of sinners around Christ"—until the then-unknown Moody and Sankey came to his church in the summer of 1873 within a few days of the inauspicious start of the campaign that was to sweep England. . . . Through Moody [Meyer] "learned how to point men to God."
>
> Next year he attended the Oxford Conference. His spiritual life . . . remained "spasmodic and fitful"—until C. T. Studd and Stanley Smith of the Cambridge Seven visited Leicester in November, 1884, when Meyer was thirty-seven. "I saw that these young men had something which I had not, but which was to them a constant source of rest and joy." At seven in the morning following their meeting, he called round to their lodgings to find they had already been long at their Bibles. Meyer asked, "How can I be like you?"
>
> Charlie Studd enquired if Meyer had ever "given yourself to Christ, for Christ to *fill* you?"
>
> "Yes, in a general sort of way, but I don't know that I have done it particularly."
>
> The talk that the three had then Meyer called "one of the formative influences of my life."[4]

Three years later, F. B. Meyer visited the Keswick Convention in Cumberland, still retaining a strong consciousness of inward poverty. One evening after the close of the official meeting . . . Meyer crept "under the tent" and walked into the night up Manor Brow and toward the high ground, feeling "the time had come when I must get everything or have a broken heart." He "walked to and fro, and said to God: 'I must have the best; I cannot go on living like this.'"

He seemed to hear God's voice to his soul, "Breathe in the air, breathe it in, and as you breathe it into your lungs, let there be an intake from God." . . .

Then Meyer remembered the words of C. T. Studd in their talk three years earlier, and spoke again to his Lord: "I am not willing, but I am willing to be made willing." In the quiet of the hillside he *opened his whole being*.

He felt no surge of feeling, so that George Grubb later that night doubted the validity of the experience. Meyer disagreed: "Though I do not feel it, I reckon God is faithful."[5]

Meyer had capitulated to Christ and had handed over the keys to every room of his life. Thereafter he became the Spirit-filled man who wrote *The Christ-Life for the Self-Life*.

As I have observed, one of the saddest facts about Christian churches today is that Christ is Guest, but He's not Host. We must own Him as Host: He must become Head of the table. Prevalent false teaching suggests that by making Christ totally Lord, we negate the distinctiveness of our personalities. That is not true. God makes originals. He does not make duplicates. He wants us to be our unique and renewed selves in Jesus Christ. The text says, "It is no longer I who live, but Christ lives in *me.*" Yes, I still retain my personhood, but now I reflect the Lord Jesus Christ like nobody else.

All the difference in the world separates between knowing Christ as Guest and knowing Christ as Host. That is why Paul prays in Ephesians 3:16–17 "that He would grant you, according to the riches of His glory, to be strengthened with might through His Spirit in the inner man, that Christ may dwell in your hearts through faith." The church at Ephesus was a mature body of believers, yet Paul prayed for them to be strengthened in order to appreciate the wonder of Christ's indwelling.

Dr. Handley Moule points out that the word *dwell* means "a settled residence"[6]—to be at home. The idea has a royal ring to it. The sovereign Christ must reign as "a Master resident in His proper home."[7] So Paul's longing for the saints at Ephesus was that Christ might be at home in their lives. With so many of us, Christ is in the house, but He's not "at home." We still have doors marked "Strictly Private."

My ministry compels me to live a good deal of my time in other people's houses. Quite naturally, therefore, I sample different types of hospitality. On some occasions I have been made to feel miserably out of place! In such instances I have found refuge in my bedroom or some cold, uninviting lounge. In most houses, however, I am at home at once. I know that if I needed to, I would be welcome in *any* room of the house. There is a complete absence of suspicion, strain, and stress. In addition, there is the delightful restfulness of being wanted, loved, and understood. That is the difference between being *in* the house and being *at home.*

This is precisely why Paul emphasizes "that Christ may dwell in your hearts [by] faith" (Eph. 3:17). Where there is faith, there is mutual trust and, therefore, nothing to fear. What is true in human relationships is even more meaningful in the divine relationship with Christ. When He dwells in our hearts by faith, we have quiet joy and rest. When this is not so, it is an evidence of sin in our lives. That is why Paul says, "Whatever is not [of] faith is sin" (Rom. 14:23).

Is Jesus "at home" in your life, or are there some rooms marked "Private" where Christ would not be welcome? What is even more important, is the Lord Jesus HOST in your life, or is He still only that tolerated GUEST?

When Peter presents this truth, he uses the imperative and writes, "In your hearts reverence Christ as Lord" (1 Pet. 3:15, RSV). Yes, He must be given the best room in the house—which is the heart—and complete headship in the home, which is the life. Only then can the believer affirm, "Christ lives in me" (Gal. 2:20).

We have been thinking of the miracle of His indwelling, through the operation and revelation of the Holy Spirit, but there is something more:

The Mastery of Christ's Indwelling

When we say, "Christ lives in me" (Gal. 2:20), it means more than the miracle and measure of His indwelling. It denotes the mastery of His indwelling. Paul had to state, "Christ lives in me," (Gal. 2:20) before he could declare, "For to me to live is Christ" (Phil. 1:21). In that phrase he sums up the whole of Christian experience. In that one comprehensive utterance is gathered up life FROM Christ, life WITH Christ, life IN Christ, and life FOR Christ. Paul, in effect, is affirming that "living IS Christ," which parallels the statement that "Christ . . . is our life" (Col. 3:4).

The title "Christ," when used in this context, must always be associated with the fact that our Messiah is anointed Prophet, Priest, and King. If Christ is living in you and me, He must dwell in more than just certain rooms. He must be the only Spokesman in our lives as Prophet; He must be the only Savior in our lives as Priest; He must be the only Sovereign in our lives as King.

As Prophet, Priest, and King, He gives *the mastery of a life of victory*. Paul exclaims, "Thanks be to God, who gives us [present tense] the victory through our Lord Jesus Christ" (1 Cor. 15:57). The victorious Christian life is the life of the victorious Christ living within. It is more than a philosophy, more than an idea, more than some wider, higher, or deeper doctrinal emphasis. *The victorious life is the victorious Lord living in you and me in utter mastery.*

Victory over what? Victory over *the world*. Jesus said, "Be of good cheer, I have overcome the world" (John 16:33). If He has overcome the world and is continuing to overcome the world, He can overcome the world in you and me now. You say, "What is the world?" Let there be no debate or doubt about it.

The world is "the lust of the flesh, the lust of the eyes, and the pride of life" (1 John 2:15–17). If Christ is indwelling us now, then we can know victory over lustful affections, victory over lustful attractions, and victory over lustful ambitions.

What about *lustful affections*—"the lust of the flesh" (1 John 2:16)? A pastor whose name is a buzzword all across this country said in a pulpit in my hearing, "When I look at my congregation and I see pretty blonde girls, I lust after them even while I preach." Preachers are falling morally every week. Charles Colson in his book *The Body* states that "the divorce rate among clergy is increasing faster than in any other profession. Numbers show that one in ten have had an affair with a member of their congregation, and 25 percent have had illicit sexual contact."[8] One is heartbroken to hear of men who have mistresses within their own congregations. It is even more alarming to learn that when preachers are excommunicated from one church, they are embraced and welcomed in the next. If that is true of the clergy, what shall we say of the average church member?

Let me ask another question: Have you celebrated victory over *lustful attractions*—"the lust of the eyes" (1 John 2:16)? How many hours do you spend at your television set as against the time you devote to your Bible, your study books, and things that are "lovely" and "praiseworthy" (Phil. 4:8)? What about your eyes? Psychologists tell us that we can impact people for good or evil by a look! One look of the Savior's eyes brought Peter to his knees in repentance, contrition, and uncontrollable weeping. How do you affect the people you meet face to face every day?

If I were to go to your home and ransack your shelves, would I find a pile of pornographic literature? Is it possible that you are out of harmony with your spouse and, therefore, not living together? As a consequence, you are satisfying yourself by looking at X-rated movies. You are the first one to go into an airport bookstall and pick up magazines you know you shouldn't even touch.

"The lust of the eyes" is supremely the problem of greed. We all want what we see! Herein is the genius of Madison Avenue marketing and advertising. The United States thrives on it.

Vance Havner tells of the time he brought a saintly friend of his from the deep South to New York City for a weekend "treat." Havner showed him all the sights, as well as the shops around Rockefeller Center. At the end of the day Dr. Havner asked his friend what he thought of it all. After a moment's reflection, the old Christian warrior simply said, "Well, I've seen it all; but, quite honestly, there isn't anything I've seen that I can't live without!"

What about *lustful ambitions*—"the pride of life" (1 John 2:16)? For your own glory you *want* to be the president of your denomination or business affiliation; you *want* to be the celebrity in the orbit of your universe; you *want* to call the shots. This can be true in the home, the church, the community, and the world. Prominence is not wrong—*if God exalts you*. On the other hand, it is written, "God resists the proud, but gives grace to the humble" (James 4:6). It is a solemn thing to be mastered and motivated by lustful ambitions.

Have you victory over *the flesh?* We read that Jesus "condemned sin in the flesh" (Rom. 8:3). The danger for Christians is that of morbid introspection. "God . . . sending His own Son in the likeness of sinful flesh . . . condemned sin in the flesh" (Rom. 8:3) that we might fulfill the righteous requirements of the law according to the Spirit. Yes, He has condemned sin in the flesh and has crucified it once and for all. But instead of examining ourselves (in a healthy manner) to see whether fellowship is broken and, if so, quickly seeking restoration on the basis of 1 John 1:9, we go down to the cemetery and dig up the decomposing bones of a buried life. In other words, we make "provision for the flesh, to fulfill its lusts" (Rom. 13:14).

Not only must there be victory over the world and the flesh, there must be victory over *the devil.* Let's not fool ourselves—the devil is real and on his last rampage before Jesus Christ comes back. His demons are working overtime to trip up God's people. The Bible says, "We do not wrestle against flesh and blood, but against principalities, against powers, against the rulers of the darkness of this age, against spiritual hosts of wickedness in the heavenly places" (Eph. 6:12). John tells us that the Christ who indwells us is "greater than he who is in the world" (1 John 4:4). To quote John again: "The Son of God was manifested that He might destroy the works of the devil" (1 John 3:8). Do you know victory over the devil?

I was brought up on the mission field in Africa by a devout father from the Christian Brethren tradition. I saw him exorcise demons from witch doctors. One such man was converted and later became a great evangelist, but on no occasion did *he* presume to rebuke the devil. Who are we to rebuke the devil?

Even Michael the archangel of heaven wouldn't rebuke the devil. The archangel said, "The Lord rebuke you!" (Jude 9). But we can exercise daring faith by trusting the indwelling Son of God in all His omnipotence to rebuke the devil every time he attacks us.

The Puritans had no illusions about the subtlety or strength of the enemy. Here is one of their prayers:

> O Lord,
>
> I bless thee that the issue of the battle between thyself and Satan has never been uncertain and will end in victory.
>
> Calvary broke the dragon's head, and I contend with a vanquished foe, who with all his subtlety and strength has already been overcome.
>
> When I feel the serpent at my heel, may I remember him whose heel was bruised, but who, when bruised, broke the devil's head.
>
> My soul with inward joy extols the mighty conqueror.
>
> Heal me of any wounds received in the great conflict;
> if I have gathered defilement,
> if my faith has suffered damage,
> if my hope is less than bright,
> if my love is not fervent,
> if some creature-comfort occupies my heart,
> if my soul sinks under the pressure of the fight.
>
> O thou whose every promise is balm, whose every touch is life, draw near to thy weary warrior; refresh me that I may

rise again to wage the strife and never tire until my enemy is
trodden down.

Give me such fellowship with thee that I may defy Satan,
unbelief, the flesh, the world, with delight that comes not
from a creature and which a creature cannot mar.

Give me a draught of the eternal fountain that lieth in thy
immutable, everlasting love and decree.

Then shall my hand never weaken, my feet never stum-
ble, my sword never rest, my shield never rust, my helmet
never shatter, my breastplate never fall, as my strength rests
in the power of thy might.[9]

The mastery of a life of victory must be matched by *the mastery of a life of purity*. Paul reminds us that Christ in us is "the *hope
of glory*" (Col. 1:27). Why "the hope of glory"? Because one of
the great provisions for purity is the hope of Christ's return. As
children of God, we don't know what we're going to be, but "we
[do] know that when He is revealed, we shall be like Him, for
we shall see Him as He is. And everyone who has this hope in
Him purifies himself, just as He is pure" (1 John 3:2–3). We are
not told the date when Jesus will return, but we should be living as if He died yesterday, rose today, and is coming back
tomorrow. We should be *loving* His appearing—in contrast to
Demas who "loved this present world" (2 Tim. 4:8-10). Nobody
living in the light of His coming again will pursue an impure life.

Here, then, is the mastery of a life of purity. How can we sin
when the pure One lives in our hearts? If Joseph were living
today and facing the same fierce temptation to fall to the seduc-
tions of a wicked woman, I am sure his language would be

something like this: "How then can I do this great wickedness, and sin against God [with Jesus in my heart]?" (Gen. 39:9).

Finally, there must be *the mastery of a life of energy.* "Christ in [us], the hope of glory" (Col. 1:27) carries the surge of energy that will one day result in the full possession of our resurrection bodies. A present application to that verse is found in Romans 8:11 where we are informed that the Spirit that quickened the Lord Jesus from the dead "will also give life to [our] mortal bodies." Surely, the Holy Spirit is going to be active in the resurrection of the saints; but there is a dynamism, a renewal, an energy we can experience *here and now.* Paul tells us all about that divine energy in Philippians 4:13: "I can do all things through Christ who strengthens me." J. B. Phillips puts it this way: "I am ready for anything through the strength [the power, the *dynamis*] of the One who lives within me."

Some years ago I went to tea at a friend's house. In the course of our conversation, he learned that I had been an engineer and loved tinkering with cars. Before long he took me to the back of his garden where he had a workshop. He showed me things he had crafted, pieces of brilliant workmanship. I asked, "How do you produce work like this?"

With a grin of satisfaction on his face, he said, "Here's my secret," and he unveiled his precious lathe. Then with a flourish of his hand, he said (I'll never forget it!), "I have power laid on to do anything."

And I couldn't help remembering the words of Paul as translated by J. B. Phillips: "I am ready for anything through the strength of the One who lives within me" (Phil. 4:13).

My dear friend Alan Redpath (now in glory) used to tell of a wealthy man in South Africa who bought a Rolls Royce. He looked the car over, took it for a test drive, and was satisfied with its general performance. He had never driven anything like this ultimate in automobiles. As he was about to hand over the check, it dawned on him that the agent hadn't told him the car's horsepower. He insisted on having this information. The man replied, "Sir, I don't have that detail, but I'll try and get it for you as soon as I can." He then wired the London office, and by return telegram came this message with just two words on it: "Horsepower adequate."

What Paul is sharing with us here is that whatever comes— turmoil, triumph, good days, bad days, sorrow, or solace— whatever the circumstances, JESUS IS ADEQUATE! And so are we. Why? Because Christ lives in us.

Many years ago my wife, Heather, and I wrote a little chorus based on my life's verse, Galatians 2:20. Christians all over Britain sang the words:

> *Be Thou my life, dear Lord, I pray,*
> *Dwell in my heart by faith alway;*
> *O'er my whole being have full sway,*
> *That I may triumph day by day.*

So we have looked at the miracle of His indwelling, the measure of His indwelling, and the mastery of His indwelling. My prayer is that you and I may experience the victory, purity, and energy of the Holy Spirit, who makes Jesus real in us. The *Old Sarum Primer* of 1558 expresses it elegantly:

> *God be in my head, and in my understanding;*
> *God be in mine eyes, and in my looking;*
> *God be in my mouth, and in my speaking;*
> *God be in my heart, and in my thinking;*
> *God be at mine end, and at my departing.*

For Further Study

1. Why are Christians sometimes afraid to let the indwelling Christ be their Lord? What keeps you from allowing Him to rule in your life? What rooms do you not want Him to enter? Why? Are you willing to talk to Him about this?

2. What is the difference between Christ being revealed *to* us and *in* us? How did this difference affect the life and ministry of the Apostle Paul (see Acts 9:6; Galatians 1:15-16)? Have you experienced this? Are you keenly aware of Christ's presence in your life today?

3. Is Christ only a Guest in your life, or is He also its Host (see Revelation 3:20)? What does this mean, in your own words? Committed to the Word or conformed to the world—which best describes you (see Romans 12:2)? If a change is needed, what will you do to see that come about?

4. Does Christ "dwell in your heart through faith" (Ephesians 3:16-17)? Is He truly at home there? Why or why not?

5. Is Christ Prophet, Priest, and King in your life? What more does Christ want to do in your life as Prophet . . . as Priest . . . as King?

6. What does purity have to do with Christ's indwelling the believer? And what does His promised return have to do with purity? What are you doing in your life to remain pure even as He is pure?

Chapter Four

Not I, But Christ
and
His Faith

Now faith is the substance of things hoped for, the evidence of things not seen. For by it the elders obtained a good testimony.

By faith we understand that the worlds were framed by the word of God, so that the things which are seen were not made of things which are visible.

By faith Abel offered to God a more excellent sacrifice than Cain, through which he obtained witness that he was righteous, God testifying of his gifts; and through it he being dead still speaks.

By faith Enoch was translated so that he did not see death, "and was not found because God had translated him"; for before his translation he had this testimony, that he pleased God.

But without faith it is impossible to please Him, for he who comes to God must believe that He is, and that He is a rewarder of those who diligently seek Him.

HEBREWS 11:1–6

Therefore we also, since we are surrounded by so great a cloud of witnesses, let us lay aside every weight, and the sin which so easily ensnares us, and let us run with endurance the race that is set before us, looking unto Jesus, the author and finisher of our faith, who for the joy that was set before Him endured the cross, despising the shame, and has sat down at the right hand of the throne of God.

For consider Him who endured such hostility from sinners against Himself, lest you become weary and discouraged in your souls.

HEBREWS 12:1–3

Chapter Four

Not I, But Christ and His Faith

I live by faith in the Son of God.

GALATIANS 2:20

O
ur study of Galatians 2:20 started with the subject "Not I, but Christ." Then we looked at "Not I, but Christ and His Death," followed by "Not I, but Christ and His Life." Now we focus on the faith that makes the death and life of Christ a personal reality. The text reads, "I live by faith in the Son of God" (v. 20). The better rendering is "in faith, the faith which is in the Son of God."[1] Dr. Handley Moule puts it, "faith steeped in the Son of God." This trusting life in the Son of God and our identification with Him in death and resurrection calls for:

An Objective Faith in Christ

Paul expresses it as "the faith which is in the Son of God" (Gal. 2:20). Now people everywhere have some kind of faith. It's nothing comparable to the faith addressed in this chapter, but all of us have some measure of faith. What is more, the strength or weakness of faith depends upon the object in which it is reposed. In our text, objective faith is in the Son of God. Because of who He is—God of very God—we can trust Him. The more we trust Him, the more faith becomes progressive until, eventually, it is enthroned in glory!

Now to guard this objective faith, the New Testament stipulates two qualifications. First, it must be *"unfeigned faith."* Writing to Timothy, the apostle tells him, "The end of the commandment is [love] out of a pure heart, and of a good conscience, and of faith unfeigned" (1 Tim. 1:5, KJV). Now the word *feigned* is interesting. It refers to actors who pretend to be something they are not. They are performing. We so easily pretend or feign faith in the Son of God until some breakdown—moral, mental, or physical—brings us to the sense of our own unreality!

Think of Peter. The wheat of Peter's faith was so mixed with the chaff of sham and unreality that the Lord allowed him to pass through the fires of denial, cursing, and swearing until, utterly broken and totally repentant, he was restored. Jesus said, "Satan has asked for you [plural—that is, all the disciples], that he may sift you [plural] as wheat. But I have prayed for you [singular], that *your faith* should not fail" (Luke 22:31–32). Because Peter was prayed for, his faith did not fail. That's why he could talk about "precious faith" in writing his epistle (1 Pet. 1:7).

One wonders as we see the days of Noah and Lot repeated in our time whether the Son of Man will find real faith on the earth when He comes (Luke 18:8; see context 17:26-37). We consider ourselves men and women of faith, but is it unfeigned faith—or are we playacting? Is it a charade?

The Bible calls for unfeigned faith, but also for *unwavering faith.* Weigh carefully the practical words of James when he speaks of our approach to God: "Ask in faith, with no doubting [no wavering]" (James 1:6). If we look at ourselves, we have cause to waver. If we look at the devil, we tremble. But when we repose our faith in the Son of God, we have reason to trust— for He cannot fail.

When I fear my faith will fail, Christ will hold me fast;
When the tempter would prevail, He can hold me fast.

I could never keep my hold, He must hold me fast;
For my love is often cold, He must hold me fast.

Ada R. Habershon

Hudson Taylor learned this secret early in his missionary work. At the time when he was revising the New Testament into the Ningpo dialect, he came upon those words in Mark 11:22: "Have faith in God." Looking at the Greek, he said to himself, "Surely that could be translated, 'Hold the faithfulness of God.'" This insight not only revolutionized his own life, but affected his entire ministry as well.[2]

You see, our part in the exercise of faith is not to strive to create or develop faith, but to hold fast the faithfulness of God. The wonder of it all is that when our faith fails or even falters, "He remains faithful; He cannot deny Himself" (2 Tim. 2:13). How important then to read God's Word daily in our quiet times and to study the Scriptures for sermon preparation so that our faith grows! "Faith comes by hearing, and hearing by the word of God" (Rom. 10:17).

But in addition to an objective faith in the Son of God, the text calls for:

A Responsive Faith in Christ

"The life which I now live in the flesh I live by faith in the Son of God" (Gal. 2:20). The more we realize the trustworthiness of our Savior and His Word, the more we want to appropriate His life in all its fullness. Objective faith *in* Him becomes responsive faith *to* Him. This response of faith can be summed up in three phrases that capture the Christian life from beginning to end.

First, there must be *the taking of Christ.* John tells us that "as many as received Him, to them He gave the right to become children of God, even to those who believe in His name" (John 1:12). The word *take* conveys the idea behind those frequently recurring New Testament verbs *believe* and *receive.* Together with the noun *faith,* they are used five hundred times in the New Testament. For the most part, they are covered by that little word *take. Believing the truth of Christ is taking Christ at His Word; receiving the gift of Christ is taking Christ at His worth.* The faith that takes is the faith that draws moment by moment on the promises and provisions of the indwelling Son of God. Every time we take, Christ undertakes.

Many years ago a number of Christian men, including F. B. Meyer, were spending an autumn evening around the fire in the study of the late Canon Wilberforce. They were discussing the problem of the inner life. After one or two had spoken about negative temptation, an elderly clergyman stood up and said, "I am naturally of a very irascible temper. When addressing the children of my Sunday school recently, they were more than usually restless. I was on the point of losing my temper, but was led to look up, and I saw the Savior standing there, so calm and sweet and strong that I felt led to say, 'Lord, give me Thy patience, for mine is giving out.' At once, He seemed to drop into my heart a lump of His own patience, and I could have stood twice as many children and twice as much inattention without losing myself. From that moment, I have followed the same method. When tempted to pride, I have said, 'Thy humility, Lord.' In temptations to quick temper, I have said, 'Thy patience, Lord.' Thus temptation has become to me a positive means of grace."[3]

A. B. Simpson was a Presbyterian minister before he launched the Christian and Missionary Alliance. He made New York audiences come alive with the message of the indwelling life of Christ as he preached Sunday afternoons in his "Victory Hour." In a personal testimony he writes:

> I shall never forget the morning that I spent in my church reading an old musty book I had discovered in my library on the subject, "The Higher Christian Life." As I pored over that little volume, I saw a new light. The Lord Jesus revealed Himself as a living, all-sufficient Presence, and I learned for the first time that Christ had not saved us from future peril and left us to fight the battle of life as best we could; but He who had justified us was waiting to sanctify us, to enter into our spirit, and substitute His strength, His holiness, His joy, His love, His faith, His power for all our worthlessness, helplessness and nothingness, and make it an actual living fact. "I live; yet not I, but Christ liveth in me" (Gal. 2:20). It was indeed a new revelation. Throwing myself at the feet of the glorious Master, I claimed the mighty promise—"I will dwell in them, and walk in them" (2 Cor. 6:16).[4]

This concept of appropriating faith was beautifully captured in one of his many hymns:

I clasp the hand of Love divine,
I claim the gracious promise mine,
And add to His my countersign,
"I take"—"He undertakes."

That's responsive faith.

But we must go further. Faith means more than the taking of Christ: it means *the yielding to Christ.* In his introduction to Romans, Paul speaks of "obedience to the faith among all nations" (Rom. 1:5). The apostle is showing here that obedience issues from faith (the act of assent or surrender). If Christ is living in our hearts by faith, then moment by moment we yield to Him. Indeed, one clear evidence that we possess a living faith is that we are constantly yielding to Christ as our indwelling Lord. This is why Paul exhorts, "Present yourselves to God as being alive from the dead," and then he adds, "To whom you present yourselves slaves to obey, you are that one's slaves" (Rom. 6:13, 16).

Some time ago a young man came up to me after a service and said, "I never realized that the life I am to live as a Christian is not achieved through striving to *copy* an historical Christ who lived two thousand years ago. Rather, it is trusting Jesus to live out His life in me *as I surrender to Him in disciplined obedience.*" Then he added, "I worked with an organization for many years, from which I have now resigned. They taught a pietistic theology that requires nothing but simple faith from me: Jesus does it all!"

"That's only half the truth!" I replied. "The taking of Christ must be matched by the yielding to Christ, and that calls for *discipline, obedience, dedication, and self-giving*. This is not passivity; this is action. He is your life, and you are to obey His indwelling presence and control."

Obedience is the indispensable word in the Christian's vocabulary. Dr. Carl Henry has said that "the greatest sin of the evangelical church today is unapplied orthodoxy"; and Dr. Alan Redpath has observed that "it is not more truth that we need today, but obedience to the truth we already know." It involves yielding to the sovereign Lord moment by moment. When He wants my hands, I yield my hands. When He wants my feet, I yield my feet. When He wants my eyes, I yield my eyes. When He wants my lips, I yield my lips. When He wants my heart, I say, "There it is, Lord. Pump Your love through it in terms of my behavior patterns." When He wants the outshining of glory, I say, "Lord, here's a poor, broken body, but flesh out Your glory through it."

In my younger years I wanted to be a surgeon; I loved watching surgery (an art form of the first order!). When I held citywide crusades in Manchester, England, I often visited a well-known hospital to watch my good friend operate. Dr. Robert Wyse was one of England's greatest surgeons. With fascination I studied his hands as he sutured the cleft palate of a baby to transform the contorted face into something beautiful. What impressed me was the team of assisting surgeons and nurses who anticipated all his needs without a single word. When the surgeon lifted his hand, the nurse was ready with the scalpel or suture— or whatever else was required at that moment. Not once was there a word between them as the operation proceeded—just total readiness and yieldedness.

Surely, this is the sense of Paul's words: "Present yourselves to God as being alive from the dead, and your members as instruments of righteousness to God" (Rom. 6:13). When Jesus wants a hand, it is there. When He wants a voice, it is there. This is yielding faith, living by faith in the Son of God in such close communion that whatever God wants is available.

But responsive faith involves not only the taking of Christ, the yielding to Christ, but also *the resting in Christ*. In Psalm 37:7 the psalmist exhorts, "Rest in the Lord, and wait patiently for Him." In the Hebrew, the word *rest* virtually means "quit nagging," "be silent to the Lord." When we have reached that ultimate communion with the indwelling Lord Jesus Christ, we know how to appropriate divine life, taking from Him all that we need. We need not nag Him. We simply rest in Him and in His gracious purpose for our lives.

Heather and I have been married forty-six years. Some of the most precious moments we have had together, whether driving, looking out a window onto a seascape, or sometimes sitting by a log fire reading quietly, have been times of "understood silence." We are at rest in one another's presence. Needless to say, meaningful vibes were going back and forth! That's what "the rest of faith" is all about. This phrase may not be in Scripture, but it's a mighty truth! George Eliot put it this way: "Friendship is the inexpressible comfort of feeling safe with a person, having neither to weigh thoughts nor measure words."

The Greek scholar W. E. Vine points out that the word *faith* includes the idea of "a personal surrender to [God] (John 1:12)" and "a conduct inspired by such surrender."[5] In essence, the noun *faith* means the leaning of the entire human personality upon God.

Will Houghton in *The Living Christ* illustrates the principle of faith from the life of John Paton, a missionary to the New Hebrides. Paton translated the Gospel of John into the national language. It took him some time to find an equivalent for the word *believe*, and he was almost at the point of frustration. One day a field hand came into his office, and, sitting down in one chair with his feet upon another, he exclaimed, "Oh, I'm so tired. I must lean my whole weight on these two chairs." Paton was jubilant. "Praise the Lord, I have my word!" Every time he used the terms *believe* or *faith*, he put in the word that meant "I am resting my whole weight upon."[6] That is rest.

Do you know what it means to rest in the Lord? This is what is implied by "I live by faith in the Son of God, who loved me and gave Himself for me" (Gal. 2:20).

When our Lord was here upon earth, He lived every moment by faith in God through dependence on the Holy Spirit. If He needed to do this, how much more you and I. "He who has entered His rest has himself also ceased from his [own] works" (Heb. 4:10). In Matthew 11:28-29 the Master said, "Come to Me, all you who labor and are heavy laden, and I will *give you rest*." Then He added, "Take My yoke upon you and learn from Me . . . and you will *find rest* for your souls." Here we have a *given* rest as well as a *found* rest. Most of us know the first rest, but not too many know the second rest. It's the same differentiation we make when we talk about "peace with God" and "the peace of God" that guards our hearts and minds in Christ Jesus. I echo the words of Eliza H. Hamilton:

> *My Saviour, Thou hast offered rest:*
> *Oh, give it then to me;*
> *The rest of ceasing from myself,*
> *To find my all in Thee.*

In a similar vein is that chorus written by Jean Sophia Pigott:

> *Jesus, I am resting, resting,*
> *In the joy of what Thou art;*
> *I am finding out the greatness*
> *Of Thy loving heart.*

So to "live by faith in the Son of God" (Gal. 2:20) is to take of Him, yield to Him, and rest in Him. Whenever such faith is *not* exercised, there is SIN in the life, for "whatever is not from faith is sin" (Rom. 14:23).

Once more, our text suggests:

A Progressive Faith in Christ

"I live by faith in the Son of God, who loved me and gave Himself for me" (Gal. 2:20). In the last analysis, the faith of which the apostle speaks in this verse is not our faith but the faith of the Son of God. The verse could be translated as follows: "I live steeped in the faith of the Son of God, who loved me and delivered Himself up for me" (Gal. 2:20). Paul here is speaking of faith as the element in which the Christian lives and grows. *This is the progressive faith that develops out of an objective faith in and a responsive faith to the Son of God.* Faith undergoes a transformation by its very union with the indwelling Son of God. As we look off to *Jesus,* our faith becomes more and more like His. Paul implies this progression of faith when he speaks of the saving power of the gospel that leads us "from faith to faith" (Rom. 1:17).

A number of Bible references illustrate this progression of faith. When the disciples became fearful in a storm despite the presence of the Lord Jesus, He had to ask, "How is it that you have *no faith?*" (Mark 4:40). On another occasion, when teaching His followers about the providence and provision of an all-caring God, Jesus had to gently rebuke them with the words, "O you of *little faith*" (Luke 12:28). The point is that these men weren't prepared to trust their Heavenly Father.

Then Jesus encountered a Roman centurion. The officer demonstrated such an understanding of the divine authority of the Son of God that the Master had to comment, "I have not found such *great faith,* not even in Israel!" (Matt. 8:10).

So we have here the progression from "no faith" to "little faith" to "great faith."

But the supreme example of *total faith* is our Lord Jesus Christ. The writer to the Hebrews speaks of this when he calls us to "look [off] unto Jesus, the author and finisher of our faith, who for the *joy* that was set before Him endured the cross, despising the shame, and has sat down at the right hand of the throne of God" (Heb. 12:2). Here is progressive faith at its highest and best.

Such faith is characterized by *divine ecstasy*—"Jesus, the author and finisher of . . . faith, who for the joy . . . set before Him" (Heb. 12:2). Charles Wesley superbly defines the radiant aspect of this progressive faith:

> *Faith, mighty faith, the promise sees*
> *And looks to that alone;*
> *Laughs at impossibilities*
> *And cries, "It shall be done!"*

The joy in the Savior's heart doubtless rose from bringing satisfaction to God, in the first place, and then from bringing salvation to humanity. Even the cross with all its sorrow and shame could not suppress the joy of radiant faith that abounded within His soul. In a similar way, nothing can rob us of the joy of radiant faith if it has become transformed by the Son of God. Such faith finds its supreme joy in bringing satisfaction to God and salvation to you and me. Without this quality of faith "it is impossible to please [God]" (Heb. 11:6).

Such faith is also characterized by *divine constancy*—"Jesus, the author and finisher of . . . faith . . . *endured* the cross, despising the shame" (Heb. 12:2). This faith never falters nor fails even though it has to face suffering and shame.

In *Pilgrim's Progress* Christian "espied two lions in the way" when he approached the entrance to the House Beautiful. How this must have tempted him to retreat, especially after hearing what Timorous and Mistrust had to say about the lions. But in constancy of faith Christian pressed on, enduring the frightening roars and despising the scorching breath of the fierce beasts. His assurance was the word of the House Porter who said, "Fear not the lions, for they are chained and are placed there for the trial of faith."

So it is for you and me. Lions are placed along the pathway of our pilgrim journey to test the quality of our faith. Let us never forget that Jesus has gone ahead of us to chain the lions. He also returns to take us through the ordeal, thus developing in us and through us the constancy of progressive faith.

Such faith is further characterized by *divine victory*. Having become "the author and finisher of . . . faith," Jesus "has sat down at the right hand of *the throne of God*" (Heb. 12:2). Here is the ultimate victory of progressive faith. The Lord Jesus Himself promises to every *faith*-overcomer this place of permanence. Heed this promise: "To him who overcomes I will grant to sit with Me on My throne, as I also overcame and sat down with My Father on His throne" (Rev. 3:21). And John reminds his readers that "this is the victory that has overcome . . .—our faith" (1 John 5:4).

The heroes of Hebrews 11 are not remembered so much for their words, deeds, or gifts, but for their triumphant faith. However much *human* faith may give way to sight at the appearing of our Lord, the faith that has been transformed by the indwelling Christ will endure. Paul says that whatever else may pass away, *faith abides* (1 Cor. 13:13). When Paul writes, "And now these three remain: faith, hope and love" (NIV), he is referring to eternity. "By faith and hope remaining in eternity, Paul means that trust (*pistis*) in the Lord begun in this life will continue forever. . . . Paul has alluded to a special faith in [Rev. 22:2]; now he expands it into an ongoing . . . faith . . . in an eternal God."[7]

Moreover, everyone who has truly lived by faith in the Son of God will be addressed with heaven's commendation: "Well done, good and faithful servant; . . . Enter into the joy of your lord" (Matt. 25:21). While the word *faithful* in the Savior's commendation means "worthy of trust, dependable, one who can be counted on, trustworthy," the clear implication is that the good servant has lived by faith in God. What an incentive this is to live by objective, responsive, and progressive faith in the indwelling Son of God!

So we have seen that the eternal exchange of our doubt for His faith leads to a daily trust in the Lord Jesus Christ "till glory shines." He triumphed by faith, and He expects us to do the same as we count on Him to develop in us and to display through us a similar faith along life's way. Thus we can sing as we journey along:

> *Simply trusting ev'ry day,*
> *Trusting through a stormy way;*
> *Even when [our] faith is small,*
> *Trusting Jesus—that is all.*

Edgar P. Stites

For Further Study

1. What does the phrase "unfeigned faith" suggest to you (see 1 Timothy 1:5)? Does this describe your faith? Why or why not?

2. What sometimes causes your faith to waver (see James 1:6)? What can you do to avoid this? Once you find yourself doubting, how can you regain a strong faith?

3. What does it really mean to *take* Christ? What is involved in believing on Him and receiving from Him (see John 1:12)? In what sense is this an ongoing reality? Why does it need to be?

4. What is the interrelationship between yielding to Christ and resting in Him (see Romans 1:5; Psalm 37:7)? Tell in your own words what each of these means. Why do you sometimes find it difficult to surrender to Christ in disciplined obedience?

5. What is the faith of the Son of God like (consider the author's suggested translation of Galatians 2:20)? What are its characteristics? What effect does His faith have on yours? How is this working itself out in your life?

6. "No faith . . . little faith . . . great faith"—which adjective most accurately describes your faith (see Mark 4:40; Luke 12:28; Matthew 8:10)? Are you satisfied with the current state of your faith? What does God want you to do in order to experience growth in this aspect of your spiritual life?

Chapter Five

Not I, But Christ
and
His Love

Though I speak with the tongues of men and of angels, but have not love, I have become as sounding brass or a clanging cymbal.

And though I have the gift of prophecy, and understand all mysteries and all knowledge, and though I have all faith, so that I could remove mountains, but have not love, I am nothing.

And though I bestow all my goods to feed the poor, and though I give my body to be burned, but have not love, it profits me nothing.

Love suffers long and is kind; love does not envy; love does not parade itself, is not puffed up; does not behave rudely, does not seek its own, is not provoked, thinks no evil; does not rejoice in iniquity, but rejoices in the truth; bears all things, believes all things, hopes all things, endures all things.

Love never fails. But whether there are prophecies, they will fail; whether there are tongues, they will cease; whether there is knowledge, it will vanish away.

For we know in part and we prophesy in part. But when that which is perfect has come, then that which is in part will be done away.

When I was a child, I spoke as a child, I understood as a child, I thought as a child; but when I became a man, I put away childish things.

For now we see in a mirror, dimly, but then face to face. Now I know in part, but then I shall know just as I also am known.

And now abide faith, hope, love, these three; but the greatest of these is love.

Pursue love.

1 CORINTHIANS 13:1—14:1a

Chapter Five

Not I, But Christ and His Love

. . . the Son of God who loved me
and gave Himself for me.

GALATIANS 2:20

JOHN HAS BEEN CALLED "THE APOSTLE OF LOVE." THIS certainly cannot be disputed when we read his Gospel and especially his three epistles. He reminds us that "we love because [God] first loved us," and then he adds, "Those who say 'I love God,' and hate their brothers or sisters, are liars" (1 John 4:19–20, NRSV). But equally powerful and profitable is the Apostle Paul's treatment of love in 1 Corinthians 13 with its relational ramifications.

A careful consideration of this teaching on love makes it convincingly evident that the greatest need in the world today is love for God and for people—that love which in the New Testament is called *agapē*. Nearly all the problems in our contemporary society would be solved if we could exchange the hate that is in us for the love that is in God.

So we come to one of the most important chapters of our study of Galatians 2:20. Paul refers to "the Son of God, who loved me and gave Himself for me." The wonder of this love does not call so much for contemplation as for dedication. The same Son of God declared, "This is My commandment, that you love one another as I have loved you" (John 15:12).

With our text before us, let us see how the Son of God

loved us and, even more importantly, how He longs to love through us.

The Son of God Loves Infinitely

We must emphasize that it is *"the Son of God* who loved" (Gal. 2:20). Such love can never be compared to the changing, failing emotions and affections of sinful men and women. This love is infinite because it is the love of *God the Son.* Here is love distinguished by *absolute perfectibility*—"Love is of God" (1 John 4:7). It does not deviate from the holy standards of righteousness and justice.

In that matchless song of love in 1 Corinthians 13, Paul sets forth the characteristics of this infinite love, both negatively and positively.

Negatively, he says that "love does not envy" (1 Cor. 13:4). Among the crying sins of the pulpit and pew today are jealousy and envy. The character assassinations between preachers and members are unconscionable. As my wife and I crisscross the world, we have been saddened again and again by the spirit of unforgiveness that often prevails between church staff and people in the congregation. Is it any wonder that revival is hindered and churches have nothing to say to the world?

"Love does not parade itself" (1 Cor. 13:4). In all my years of preaching, I have never witnessed such a spiral of "celebrity-ism" as is prevalent today. Preachers wear thousand-dollar suits, crocodile shoes, unbelievable hairdos—you name it—and the Reverend Doctor stomps onto the platform! True love does not parade itself. Modesty is love's way. Ever remember that we are the vehicles through whom the Lord Jesus Christ is manifesting His glory. Jesus did not parade Himself.

"Love . . . is not puffed up" (1 Cor. 13:4). Many preachers and laymen love to recite their credentials and their achievements. Sure, people can tell the story of God's gracious work through them and relate it with humility. But when this is done in pride, "God *resists* the proud, but gives grace to the humble" (James 4:6). If you want to know why some famous preachers with fast-growing churches are now out of the ministry today, it is usually because of pride.

Preachers and lay-leaders are not the only culprits! You and I are also included. The fable is told of two swans conversing with a bullfrog. "Have you ever seen the hidden beauties of my pond?" asked the frog.

"No," replied the swans, "we have never had anyone to guide us."

"Follow me," said the frog, as he plunged into the water and conducted the two birds on their sightseeing tour. When the swans surfaced for air, they asked the frog if he would like to see something of the beauties of the countryside. "But I cannot fly," said the frog. Then he added, "If you hold a stick in your beaks while I hang on with my mouth, you could carry me through the air and show me a world I have never seen."

The two birds agreed to this, and the journey started. They flew over hill and dale, revealing something of the glory of God's wonderful handiwork. As they came down low over a village, two shoppers happened to look up and see this astonishing sight. "Isn't that clever!" remarked one of them.

"Yes," replied the other, "I wonder who thought of that?"

The frog exclaimed, "I did!" and instantly dropped to the ground. "Pride comes before a fall" is indeed what the Bible teaches (see Prov. 29:23).

"Love . . . does not behave rudely" (1 Cor. 13:4, 5). Courtesy and chivalry are not merely a matter of birth; they are a matter of the heart. It is well said that "what breeding does by training, love does by instinct." I am not irreverent to note that "the Lord Jesus was a perfect Gentleman" (David Livingstone). He was a Gentleman who did things gently and lovingly with a view to pleasing His Father (see John 8:29).

"Love . . . does not seek its own" (1 Cor. 13:4, 5). Love is not possessive—even in the pulpit. One of the reasons preachers burn out is because of a subtle possessiveness. They do not build up the saints for the work of the ministry, and they do not delegate responsibilities to others. If they did, they could give themselves wholly to the study of the Word and the practice of prayer. Instead, they insist on hogging everything themselves. Because of insecurity, perfectionism, or selfishness they refuse to involve others. As a consequence, they crash right, left, and center. What is true of the church is true of the home. Possessive love destroys relationships in the home between husband and wife, parents and children. God's love is unselfish in its interests and influence.

"Love . . . is not provoked" (1 Cor. 13:4, 5). The King James Version reads, "is not *easily* provoked." The revisers have omitted the word *easily*. Some suggest (rather humorously?) that the translators did not want to offend their patron, King James VI, who was known for his explosive temper! Love never gives way to provocation, exasperation, or irritation. It is never touchy.

Dr. F. Y. Fullerton once wrote that "the crowning glory of our Lord was that He was never impatient." How exasperated He could have been amid the pressures of His busy program! He never answered back in spite of the many unpleasant things hurled at Him by friends and foes. His friends said, "He is out of His mind" (Mark 3:21). His foes added, "He has a demon and is mad. Why do you listen to Him?" (John 10:20). Yet He remained unprovoked.

"Love . . . thinks no evil" (1 Cor. 13:4, 5). Love does not keep an account of evil done and does not reckon up grievances. In this sense love is a poor mathematician. How easily the Lord Jesus could have totaled up the evil done to Him throughout that eventful day when He was led from Gethsemane to Gabbatha, and then from Gabbatha to Golgotha! But even as the nails were driven into His hands, He prayed, "Father, forgive them, for they do not know what they do" (Luke 23:34).

Have you a memory for wrongs committed against you, or have you the fervent love that "will cover a multitude of sins" (1 Pet. 4:8)?

"Love . . . does not rejoice in iniquity" (1 Cor. 13:4, 6). Moffatt's rendering is helpful here: "Love is never glad when others go wrong." This characterization of love could be illustrated again and again in the ministry of our Lord, but one example seems to sum it up. It is the picture of Jesus weeping over Jerusalem (Matt. 23:37-39). Jerusalem, of course, refers to the entire nation of Israel. The leaders had been guilty of repeated crimes. They had rejected and even killed many of God's messengers. Indeed, eventually they crucified Jesus Himself. But in spite of all this, our wonderful Savior loved them to the end. He knew that their "house" (city and temple) would be destroyed in A.D. 70 by invading Roman armies.

Here is Incarnate Love lamenting the fate of His own people. The image is of a mother bird gathering and covering her brood. It is a dramatic portrayal of love, tender care, and willingness to protect others. Israel had sinned grievously, but Jesus did not rejoice over their impending doom. On the contrary, He wept with great sorrow.

I don't know how that strikes you, but it breaks my heart. How often we lash out at the sins of the people around us, both on the national level and the personal level; but how seldom do we kneel to weep!

Positively, "love suffers long" (1 Cor. 13:4). Here is the long-suffering that waits rather than flares. How beautifully this is revealed in our Lord's answer when Peter asked Him, "Lord, how often shall my brother sin against me, and I forgive him? Up to seven times?" The Lord, with tender satire, replied, "I do not say to you, up to seven times, but up to seventy times seven" (Matt. 18:21, 22).

"Love . . . is kind" (1 Cor. 13:4). Love is always ready to consider others with a view to extending good. Have you ever noticed how much of Christ's life was spent in doing kind things, not merely good things? Think, for instance, of the occasion when He called His disciples aside to rest awhile because "there were many coming and going, and they did not even have time to eat." But no sooner had they departed into a desert place to be quiet than a multitude broke in upon their privacy. The first reaction of the disciples was to "send them away," but the Savior answered, "You give them something to eat." Then followed that wonderful miracle of the feeding of the five thousand (Mark 6:31-44).

"Love . . . rejoices in the truth" (1 Cor. 13:6). Actually, this might be rendered, "Love . . . rejoices with the truth." When truth triumphs, love rejoices. How far removed this is from the ethos of our present day! We have only to watch our daily newscasts to prove this.

Recently my wife and I attended a magnificent Holy Week presentation. Thousands attended, and the impact was tremendous. The pastor of the church gave an appropriate invitation to those present to yield to the claims of the crucified but risen Christ. Hundreds responded. This was a triumphant event, worthy of citywide coverage by the news media. But the next day there was not even a passing reference to this holy happening. Instead, the newspapers were filled with atrocious stories of murders, thefts, divorces, and drug busts! The reporting was distinctly sadistic and certainly shameful. My heart cried out, "Love . . . rejoices with the truth!"

"Love . . . bears all things" (1 Cor. 13:4, 7). Love patiently and silently endures when it has to suffer, without breaking down or telling others what it has to bear. Recall how Jesus silently endured when subjected to the accusations of false witnesses before Pilate. We read, "He answered him not one word" (Matt. 27:14).

"Love . . . believes all things" (1 Cor. 13:4, 7). The idea behind this clause has nothing to do with credibility. It is rather the absence of suspicion. Some people are always suspicious, but the love-mastered believer always puts the best construction on things.

On one occasion the Lord Jesus was sitting in the house of Simon the leper, and a sinful woman came in and stood at His feet weeping. She kneeled down to wash and wipe the Master's feet. The immediate reaction of the hard-hearted Pharisee was, "This man, if He were a prophet, would know who and what manner of woman this is who is touching Him, for she is a sinner" (Luke 7:39).

But the Savior defended her by putting the best construction on her acts of gratitude and love. Said He, "Wherever this gospel is preached in the whole world, what this woman has done will also be told as a memorial to her" (Matt. 26:13). What a rare expression of love this is today: "Love . . . believes all things" (1 Cor. 13:4, 7)!

"Love . . . hopes all things" (1 Cor. 13:4, 7). Love is always optimistic and undiscouraged. When others have long given up, love hopes on. The Lord Jesus never gave up hope for the most depraved of people. Of Him it could be said, "A bruised reed He will not break, and smoking flax He will not quench" (Matt. 12:20). How necessary is this quality of love in Christian

work! How easily we give up because of initial discourage-
ments. The Lord give us a love that is perennially optimistic!

"Love . . . endures all things" (1 Cor. 13:7). This activity of love
is the crown of all that has gone before. It represents love's victory. The writer to the Hebrews tells us that "for the joy that was
set before Him [He] endured the cross, despising the shame, and
has sat down at the right hand of the throne of God" (Heb. 12:2).
The Apostle Paul knew something of the triumph of this love,
for he could say (writing to these same Corinthians), "Being
reviled, we bless; being persecuted, we endure it; being defamed,
we entreat" (1 Cor. 4:12–13). What a wonderful portrayal of the
activity of love is this! What a standard and how unlike human
love! How our love appears as sin in light of this unsullied and
unwavering perfectibility of infinite love.

But I want you to notice not only love's absolute perfectibility but also its *absolute dependability*—"Love never fails" (1 Cor.
13:8). Even though the disciples of Christ wavered in their
affections toward their Master—betraying, forsaking, and
denying Him in one form or another—His love was unfailing.
"Having loved His own who were in the world, He loved them
to the end" (John 13:1), to the uttermost. What was true of His
love then is equally true of His love now. This unfailingness of
the Savior's love is a quality of His infinite character. And it
must be true of us if we claim that this Jesus dwells in us.

Think about the dependability of love—"love never fails"
(1 Cor. 13:8). One day C. H. Spurgeon was riding in the country when he saw a weather vane on a farmhouse. He observed
that inscribed upon that weather vane were the words, "God Is

Love." Telling his driver to stop, he stepped out of his carriage and walked over to the farmer. Pointing to the weather vane, he asked, "How dare you put up a weather vane that reads 'God Is Love,' as if God's love changes with every breeze that blows across your farmyard!"

The man replied, "Sir, you have totally misunderstood me. I put that sign up there to show that regardless of which way the wind blows, God is *still* love." What a comfort to know that—especially when you study a book like Job!

Never a day passes without hearing stories of husbands failing wives, wives failing husbands, parents failing their children, children failing their loved ones; and on and on we could go. But His love never fails. God have mercy on us for failing to love each other in this way. Despite all the problems that can come up in married life—and even in the church—love ultimately conquers.

We are told that the heathen used to say of first-century believers, "See how these Christians love one another." Nowadays television comedians crack jokes and make a spectacle of Christians, saying, "See how these Christians fight one another!"

Paul says that the believer's vital experience is Christ living in him (Phil. 1:21). This Christ is "the Son of God, who loved" (Gal. 2:20). How does the Son of God love? The answer is that the Son of God loves infinitely; but more than that:

The Son of God Loves Intimately

How careful the apostle is to indicate that "the Son of God . . . loved *me*" (Gal 2:20). He is using the personal pronoun. Even as Paul dictated these words, he recalled how unworthy he was as an object of divine love. Paul could never get over what he had done to the church of Christ. By attacking the body, he was attacking the Head, even Jesus Himself (Acts 9:5). No wonder he finishes up one of his last letters by writing, "I thank Christ Jesus our Lord who has enabled me, because He counted me faithful, putting me into the ministry, although I was formerly a blasphemer, a persecutor, and an insolent man; but I obtained mercy because I did it ignorantly in unbelief. And the grace of our Lord was exceedingly abundant, with faith and *love* which are in Christ Jesus . . . However, for this reason I obtained mercy, that in me first Jesus Christ might show all longsuffering, as a pattern to those who are going to believe on Him for everlasting life" (1 Tim. 1:12-16). Hallelujah for such a statement!

Because God loves us intimately, His love is *impartial* in all its relatedness. "In this is love, not that we loved God, but that He loved us" (1 John 4:10). We choose whom to love. Not so Jesus. In the Gospel stories we find that He loved everyone—even Judas with his traitorous heart—to the very end (John 13:1). He loved Peter with his bungling ways (Mark 9:6). He loved James with his fiery temper (Mark 3:17). He loved John with his critical spirit (Mark 9:38). Some of these men—Peter, James, and John—came closer to Him than others during those years. It wasn't because His love was partial; it was because they came closer to Him of their own will. Peter said, "I want to come closer." "No," said John, "I'm going all the way," and he laid his head upon the bosom of our Lord Jesus Christ (John 13:23).

When I was considering the pastorate of Calvary Baptist Church in New York City, I handled many considerations by telephone over a stretch of three thousand miles. I had preached in that church in 1957 and 1958. I had also conducted a number of workshops for pastors during the 1957 Billy Graham Crusade. I never thought that one day I would be called to be the pastor of that church. Shortly after my arrival, we had a wonderful installation service. Dr. Billy Graham gave the charge to the church, and Dr. Alan Redpath gave the charge to me. Billy Graham said, "Stephen, my brother, if you don't find 'the church within the church' within a period of one year, leave and shake the dust from off your feet."

One of the first battles I faced was on the issue of racial integration within our membership. I had come from Britain where we had an integrated metropolitan church. I was dismayed to discover that I had come to a segregated church. I called the church leadership together and said, "I want to make a statement. I am going to preach God's Word. I am going to believe God to send revival among us. I am going to pray unceasingly that this situation changes. *But* if we do not become an integrated church within two years, I will no longer be the pastor. This is not a threat; this is a divine mandate."

Up to that time almost 85 percent of the church had voted that no blacks be allowed as members. But God had become in me a global God. Having lived on the mission field, I could not accept discrimination in any form whatever. God gave me eyes to see everybody as souls for whom Christ died. So I began to preach, and I began to pray, and I gathered a group of like-minded people around me.

A black federal judge came to talk to me, and I shared my convictions with him. He wouldn't believe me. I invited him to stay in the church-owned hotel. He said, "You mean I can have a room in this hotel?"

I said, "I'll see to it that you have the best room."

The next day we had another talk. Then he had to go away on a case. When he returned and asked to see me, my secretary told him I was out of town. The judge thought she was merely trying to make an excuse for my not wanting to see him. She said, "The pastor is away speaking at a convention; but if you really want to know how he feels about the matter of racism, read this sermon that he is planning to preach."

The judge sat down, read the manuscript, and left convinced. "I won't need to see him," he said.

I'll never forget the night of the business meeting. That church had never been filled like it was that night. The atmosphere was absolutely electric! I stood and preached my sermon to that whole congregation and then fielded questions. I told all my deacons that they were free to speak for themselves. They were not obliged to stand with me at this point. Several men, one in particular, rose and blasted me with the most vitriolic language that could ever come out of a human mouth. It was unbelievable.

But I stood firm, and we took a vote. The result was absolutely overwhelming—only eleven against integration. Seven of those men came to me later and confessed they had come to see their stand as sinful. What of the four remaining?

Every one of them died within a year! So I'm not talking theology that I haven't practiced. It's about time we got victory over the question of race that is breaking up our country!

God's love is not only impartial, it is *individual* in all its relatedness—"the Son of God . . . loved *me*" (Gal. 2:20). This is the point of Paul's use of the personal pronoun. He knew the love of the Son of God personally. The Lord Jesus demonstrated this throughout His life, especially as He talked about His sheep. "I am the good shepherd; and I know My sheep, and am known by My own" (John 10:14).

I think of those intimate touches of the Gospel writers. Jesus loved the rich young ruler who was going to turn his back on Him and "walk into everlasting darkness" because he chose gold rather than God. Jesus loved Lazarus. Jesus loved Mary. Jesus loved Martha. He loved them personally. C. S. Lewis says, "For a man to claim 'I love all people' is a total cop-out for loving people individually."

Do you love everybody in your church *personally?* If you don't, what are you doing about it? One of the greatest hindrances to revival is unforgiveness. Loving everybody individually doesn't mean you have to *like* everyone in the sense that you share the same interests, the same games, the same hobbies, and so on. That's a different concept. This unconditional love, this New Testament *agapē* poured into our hearts by the Holy Spirit, never discriminates.

But once more let us ask the apostle, "How does the Son of God love?" Back comes the answer:

The Son of God Loves Immeasurably

"The Son of God . . . gave Himself [up] for me" (Gal. 2:20) to the very last drop of blood. Here is sacrificial love beyond all our powers to comprehend! We can only study the Scriptures and wonder as we examine every single verse concerning that immeasurable love. I want to say two things about the characteristics of immeasurable love:

First, *sacrificial love gives.* Paul says, "The Son of God . . . loved me and gave Himself [up] for me" (Gal. 2:20). In another place he says, "Christ . . . loved the church and gave Himself [up] for it" (Eph. 5:25). The very nature of love is to give and to give. "God so loved the world that He gave His only begotten Son, that whoever believes in Him should not perish but have everlasting life" (John 3:16).

Such love can be measured *materially.* In 2 Corinthians 8:9 we are told: "For you know the grace of our Lord Jesus Christ, that though He was rich, yet for your sakes He became poor, that [we] through His poverty might become rich." That eternal fact was materially expressed on earth. How? There was no room for Him at birth (Luke 2:7), there was no home for Him in life (Luke 9:58), there was no grave for Him in death. He was buried in a borrowed tomb (Luke 23:53).

This is the same Son of God you claim lives in you by faith. Do we know anything of material sacrifice? The Apostle John tells us that "whoever has this world's goods, and sees his brother in need, and shuts up his heart from him, how does the love of God abide in him?" (1 John 3:17) The way of love is the way of sacrifice at any cost.

Someone once asked a missionary and his wife laboring in a primitive part of the world if they liked their work. The man of God replied, "My wife and I do not like dirt; we have reasonably refined sensibilities. We do not like associating with ignorant, filthy, brutish people; but natural likes and dislikes have nothing to do with it. The love of Christ constrains us, and we love these people!" Those two dear children of God were sacrificing everything because the Son of God was giving Himself through them. Can that be said of your life? If not, then you know little of Calvary love.

When C. T. Studd contemplated the sacrificing love of the Son of God, he committed himself to a motto for life: "If Jesus Christ be God and died for me, then no sacrifice is too great for me to make for Him." Oh, for a similar commitment in your life and mine!

But sacrificial love can also be measured *morally*. "By this we know love, because He laid down His life for us. And we also ought to lay down our lives for [our brothers and sisters]" (1 John 3:16). No one exemplified this aspect of love for me more than my precious mother, now in heaven. I'll never forget one of the first furlough trips back to Britain as a teenager— forty-four days on a banana boat from Lobito Bay on the west coast of Africa, by way of Lisbon, Portugal. One of the sailors became seriously ill with an infectious and loathsome disease. The captain ordered that the man be placed on a mat at the stern of the ship with the intention that when no one was looking, somebody would push the sick man overboard. My mother heard about it. She went to the captain and said, "I'm a missionary. I demand, in the name of my God and the Lord Jesus Christ whom I serve, that nothing be done to that man until I finish with him. If you act otherwise, I will report you."

She washed the sick man, medicated him, and prayed for him. Day after day went by, and the man got better. The sores began to heal, and the light returned to his eyes. By the time the ship arrived in Lisbon, he was able to stand. I saw him throw his arms around my dear mother and say, "She's the only one in the world who *loved me!*" That man was saved, and we kept in touch with him for many years.

That's sacrificial love! Don't sing those little choruses about love unless you are prepared to express it in a sacrificial way. The Christ who loves is "the Son of God, who loved me and gave Himself [up upon that cross] for me" (Gal. 2:20). Watch the blood flow from His head, His hands, His feet, His side— first gushing, then flowing a little slower, until the last drop hits the sod. To that last drop of blood He loved me, and now He lives in me. Do you know anything about that kind of love?

Sacrificial love gives; but, secondly, *sacrificial love forgives.* "Let all bitterness, wrath, anger, clamor, and evil speaking be put away from you, with all malice. And be kind to one another, tenderhearted, forgiving one another, just as God in Christ also forgave you" (Eph. 4:31–32). In the light of His impending death on Calvary's cross, Jesus was forever forgiving men and women. I think of the greatest of all moments when cruelty and venom assumed the forms of men and murder, such as has never occurred in the history of the world. My precious Lord was nailed to a Roman gibbet. As that cross was lifted into place, these words came from His lips, "Father, forgive them, . . . they do not know what they do" (Luke 23:34).

Some reading this chapter have grudges and unforgiveness in their hearts, yet claim that Christ lives in them. What hypocrisy! In churches there are people who won't talk to one another, deacons who won't look at one another, pastors who won't pray with one another. Why? There's no spirit of forgiveness.

A blind boy was asked what forgiveness was. He replied, "It is the fragrance that flowers emit when trampled upon." What a beautiful thought to associate with the Savior's dying cry! Does that fragrance of forgiving love breathe from your life when you are trampled upon? If only we were more forgiving, we would slay enmity and hostility all around us!

A Christian man moved into a community with a notoriously disagreeable neighbor. When informed of the character of this individual, the Christian remarked, "If he disturbs me, I will kill him!" The statement reached the ears of the neighbor who went out of his way to torment the new settler.

But every offense was forgiven and met with love until, at last, the contentious neighbor was completely won over. "I was told he would kill me," he said, "but I didn't know he would do it with kindness."

We have seen what we mean when we speak of "the Son of God, who loved [us] and gave Himself for [us]" (Gal. 2:20). This love is infinite, intimate, and immeasurable. In and of ourselves we cannot conceive it, but we can receive it and diffuse it. Paul tells us that "the love of God has been poured out in our hearts by the Holy Spirit who was given to us" (Rom. 5:5). One ministry of the Holy Spirit is to make the love of Christ real in us and to release it through us. Let us pray that the gracious Spirit will perform this ministry in us right NOW!

A living, loving Christian is the most unanswerable argument for Christianity. Oh, that each one of us would live by faith in the indwelling Son of God who loved and who loves! Only then can we sincerely pray:

> *May the love of Jesus fill me*
> *As the waters fill the sea;*
> *Him exalting, self abasing—*
> *This is victory.*

Kate B. Wilkinson

For Further Study

1. Do you agree that nearly all the problems in our world today would be solved if God's love (*agape* love) ruled human hearts? Why isn't His love more evident in us today?

2. Which characteristics of love, as seen in 1 Corinthians 13, are most needed in your life? How are those same characteristics exemplified in our Lord Jesus Christ? What will you do to allow Him to bring those love traits into your heart and life?

3. Have you found Christ's love for you absolutely dependable and unfailing (see 1 Corinthians 13:8)? How faithful has your love for Him been? How can you spend more time meditating on His great love?

4. Is the Son of God's love truly impartial (see 1 John 4:10)? He loved Judas, but does He still love the unlovable, the most obvious sinners, those who betray Him today? What implications does this have for your life and ministry?

5. "The Son of God . . . loved *me*" (Galatians 2:20). What does the use of the personal pronoun here mean to you? Do you love others the way Christ loves you? Why or why not?

6. Does sacrificial love always give and forgive? How is this exemplified in God and in His Son (see Ephesians 5:25; John 3:16; Ephesians 4:31-32; Luke 23:34)? Do you often worship Christ in your heart, thanking Him for His great love?

Chapter Six

Not I, But Christ
and
His Grace

O foolish Galatians! Who has bewitched you that you should not obey the truth, before whose eyes Jesus Christ was clearly portrayed among you as crucified?

This only I want to learn from you: Did you receive the Spirit by the works of the law, or by the hearing of faith?

Are you so foolish? Having begun in the Spirit, are you now being made perfect by the flesh?

Have you suffered so many things in vain—if indeed it was in vain?

Therefore He who supplies the Spirit to you and works miracles among you, does He do it by the works of the law, or by the hearing of faith?—just as Abraham "believed God, and it was accounted to him for righteousness."

Therefore know that only those who are of faith are [children] of Abraham.

And the Scripture, foreseeing that God would justify the nations by faith, preached the gospel to Abraham beforehand, saying, "In you all the nations shall be blessed."

So then those who are of faith are blessed with believing Abraham.

GALATIANS 3:1-9

Chapter Six

Not I, But Christ and His Grace

*I have been crucified with Christ; it
is no longer I who live, but Christ
lives in me; and the life which I now
live in the flesh I live by faith in
the Son of God, who loved me and gave
Himself for me. I do not set aside
the grace of God; for if righteousness
comes through the law,
then Christ died in vain.*

GALATIANS 2:20-21

W E HAVE BEEN DEALING WITH THE ESSENCE OF
the gospel. I've called it "Not I, but Christ"
because Galatians 2:20, together with the sup-
porting biblical passages, spells out the truth of fullness of life
in Christ. But our key text is incomplete if we do not include
verse 21: "I do not set aside the grace of God."

The concept of "the grace of God" is redemption's *modus
operandi* which the apostle sets forth here and in such cross-
references as Romans 4 and 5. Grace stands in direct contrast
to the feverish self-efforts of the Jewish legalists in Paul's day and
of many modern Christian legalists as well. Such self-efforts to
please God virtually ignore all that grace has done to achieve
our acceptance in Christ. If our works could have worked for
our salvation, why did God send His Son to suffer and die on
the cross? The whole idea of human merit before God so

repelled the apostle that he attacked it in one form or another in all of his epistles. For example, in Ephesians he declares, "By grace you have been saved through faith, and that not of yourselves; it is the gift of God, not of works, lest anyone should boast" (Eph. 2:8-9).

Right here in our text his rebuke is devastating. Mark well his language: "O foolish Galatians! Who has bewitched you. . . . Are you so foolish? Having begun in the Spirit, are you now being made perfect by the flesh?" (Gal. 3:1, 3). He pulverizes self-induced confidence to live the Christian life in the flesh and affirms that grace commences, continues, and completes the work of redemption in the Christian. As the old hymn puts it:

> *'Tis grace hath brought [us] safe thus far,*
> *And grace will lead [us] home.*
>
> John Newton

The fact is, we cannot live the Christian life without the CHRIST-life to live the Christian life. All is of grace.

Grace Repudiates All Self-Effort in Our Lives

The apostle states, "I do not set aside the grace of God; . . . O foolish Galatians! Who has bewitched you. . . . Having begun in the Spirit, are you now being made perfect by the flesh?" (Gal. 2:21; 3:1, 3). Paul brought the gospel of the grace of God to Galatia and preached that what the Holy Spirit begins, He continues. These people were reverting to self-effort in an attempt to live the Christ-life. To Paul this was a departure from the message he had proclaimed. It also violates the way in which grace operates in our lives. So he sets out to correct this error by emphasizing two principles.

Grace makes all self-effort amount to foolishness. Weigh Paul's language: "O foolish Galatians!" (Gal. 3:1). A Christian who continues to exert self-effort in an attempt to live a supernatural life is "foolish." The word denotes the stupidity of intellectual impotence and lack of moral judgment. Indeed, Paul goes on to ask, "Who has bewitched you?" (Gal. 3:1). This metaphor is derived from the popular superstition of "the evil eye." So Paul tells these Galatian believers that they had come under the spell of the evil one himself. One of the enemy's tactics is to persuade people to live the Christian life in their own strength. The devil is so convincing and compelling that he actually bewitches people—even Christians. He literally "hoodwinks" them. If he cannot rob us of the *fact* of salvation, he will do his utmost to rob us of the *fullness* of salvation.

The author of the epistle to the Hebrews has a stern warning about this. He writes, "We must give the more earnest heed to the things we have heard, lest we drift away. For if the word spoken through angels proved steadfast, and every transgression and disobedience received a just reward, how shall we escape if we neglect *so great a salvation,* which at the first began to be spoken by the Lord, and was confirmed to us by those who heard Him, God also bearing witness both with signs and wonders, with various miracles, and gifts of the Holy Spirit, according to His own will?" (Heb. 2:1-4).

The theme in these verses is "so great salvation." Evangelists like to preach on this text, but this is primarily a message to believers. Unbelievers "reject"; believers "neglect." Neglect what? Why, the "so great salvation," not just salvation. This "so great salvation" is of such paramount importance that the tri-une Godhead is united in declaring the message of fullness in Christ to all who appropriate Him.

Notice the text: "Having at the first been spoken through the *Lord*. . . . *God* also bearing witness. . . . by gifts of the *Holy Spirit*" (Heb. 2:3b-4, ASV). God the Father, God the Son, and God the Holy Spirit join in united testimony to this "so great salvation." And yet "we" (the pronoun is emphatic) as Christian men and women "neglect" God's bountiful provision for living the Christ-life in all its fullness. By *neglecting* this "so great salvation," we are making light of it. The Greek word is used in Matthew 22:5 where invited guests made light of the king's invitation to the wedding feast for his son. The writer to the Hebrews expands on this careless attitude and costly activity by comparing "neglect" to a drifting ship on its way to destruction. So he warns: "Give the more earnest heed . . . lest we drift away" (Heb. 2:1).

"'I have neglected Thee, O God!' cried the sinning and so penitent Bishop Lancelot Andrewes in his private devotions, and Alexander Whyte adds, 'I trembled as I heard him cry it. And I have never come upon that awful word from that day to this without a shudder.' This is the cardinal sin of the Christian, and from it stems all the other sins of the saints that bring so much dishonor [to the name of the Lord]."[1]

No wonder Paul bursts out, "O foolish Galatians! Who has bewitched you. . . . Having begun in the Spirit, are you now being made perfect by the flesh?" (Gal. 3:1, 3). This "so great salvation" is never achieved; it is always received through the unmerited grace of God. As James M. Gray, former president of Moody Bible Institute, put it in his insightful hymn:

> *Naught have I gotten but what I received,*
> *Grace has bestowed it since I have believed;*
> *Boasting excluded, pride I abase—*
> *I'm only a sinner saved by grace!*

I want to make a second point about this matter of grace. Not only does grace make all self-effort amount to foolishness, but *grace makes all self-effort amount to futility.* Paul puts it pungently here. He says, "Have you suffered so many things in vain—if indeed it was in vain?" (Gal. 3:4). The *New International Version* renders it: "Have you suffered so much for nothing—if it really was for nothing?" The implication is that to continue in the flesh after beginning in the Spirit is to end up in utter futility.

Pastors and Christian leaders everywhere are throwing up their hands in frustration. They blame it on stressed-out experiences, burnouts, being too busy, and so on. Many times it has nothing at all to do with these. Self-effort is killing them, the sin of the Galatian church. If they stopped to think, they would practice time management and learn to pace themselves and program their schedules in order to give themselves "continually to prayer and to the ministry of the word" (Acts 6:4).

What we need at this hour is anointed expository preaching that brings men and women to *brokenness* and *helplessness* and, therefore, to *utter dependence* on God. The Avis philosophy ("We try harder") is fatal in the Christian life. We do not live the Christ-life by *trying*, but rather by *trusting*. *When we try, it is self-effort, and we are bewitched; when we trust, it is Spirit-effort, and we are blessed.*

I recall when this truth became a reality in personal experience. I had already surrendered my life to Jesus Christ for the Christian ministry. While I waited to start my theological training, I spent weekends preaching in local churches. Every time I opened my mouth to speak, I was haunted by the memory of past defeats. Instead of turning to the Lord for deliverance, I tried to conquer the problem by self-effort. The result was disastrous! Instead of being liberated I was paralyzed.

In desperation I went to hear a missionary on furlough give a series of studies on Romans. Expounding chapter 6, he paused to ask this question, "Is there someone here who is haunted by his past and defeated in his witness?" I knew God was speaking to me, so I listened the more intently. Then he continued, "Do you know that such *introspection* is a violation of the principle of grace? God has condemned, crucified, and buried your 'old self.' What right have you to visit the cemetery of your moral past and dig up the bones? Accept by faith what God has done and trust the Holy Spirit to liberate you to live the resurrection life in Christ." That was all I needed. I saw the foolishness and futility of self-effort, and the grace of God set me free!

Surely introspection must not be confused with the healthy self-examination we need to do when we sense that communion with God has been broken. Whenever sin interrupts fellowship with the Lord, sin must be confessed and forsaken (1 John 1:9). There and then communion is restored, and the Holy Spirit fills the life.

But let us go further:

Grace Appropriates All
Spirit-Effort in Our Lives

"Having begun in the Spirit, are you now . . . made perfect by the flesh?" (Gal. 3:3). Here is a question with tremendous implications. How God begins is how God continues and completes His work. Writing to the Philippians, Paul states the same truth: "Being confident of this very thing, that He who has begun a good work in you will complete it until the day of Jesus Christ" (Phil. 1:6).

Observe that *the Holy Spirit originates the life of Christ in us.* Those words "He who has begun a good work in you" (Phil. 1:6) take us back to the day when we were born again. The question we must ask ourselves is whether we have been born again. The consensus of discerning Christian leaders is that a large proportion of people who attend our churches have never had this regenerating experience. We are back to the days when George Whitefield, the great preacher and revivalist, visited America. He was always dwelling on this basic theme of John 3:3, whether addressing an Indian in a canoe on one of the great American rivers, or black men in the Bermudas, or an aristocratic audience in the drawing room of the Countess of Huntingdon. A friend inquired of George Whitefield, "Why do you preach so often on 'Ye must be born again?'" "Because," was his answer, "'ye must be born again!'"[2]

Bishop Taylor-Smith was preaching one Sunday to a fashionable congregation in London, England. At the morning service he took as his text the words of Jesus to Nicodemus, "Ye must be born again." After the service someone told him that they were not used to that kind of preaching in their church. It might be all right for the Salvation Army but not for a congregation such as theirs. That evening he preached again, this time on the words, "*Marvel not* that I said unto thee, 'Ye must be born again.'"[3]

This beginning of the life of Christ within the human personality is a divine miracle. Even Nicodemus (*the* teacher of Israel, John 3:10) had to learn this great lesson. No story in the Bible illustrates this more delicately than the record of Christ's birth (Luke 1:26–38). The angel came to Mary and told her that she had found favor with God. Then he announced, "Behold, you will conceive in your womb and bring forth a Son, and shall call His name Jesus."

The astonished Mary replied, "How can this be, since I do not know a man?"

The angel answered, "The Holy Spirit will come upon you, and the power of the Highest will overshadow you; therefore, . . . that Holy One who is to be born will be called the Son of God. . . . For with God nothing will be impossible."

Mary's answer is one of the most exalted utterances to be

found in Scripture. In complete submissiveness and holy expectation she exclaimed, "Behold the maidservant of the Lord! Let it be to me according to your word." And so it came to pass that she conceived and brought forth Jesus.

You and I must imitate Mary's example if we are to be indwelt by the life of the Son of God. The birth of Christ in us is wholly dependent upon the work of the Holy Spirit (John 3:6; Gal. 4:19).

Secondly, *the Holy Spirit consolidates the life of Christ in us.* When Paul asks, "Are you now being made perfect by the flesh?" (Gal. 3:3), he is implying that the vital alternative is to be *perfected by the Spirit.* Just as we need the new birth (Christ born in us), so we need the Holy Spirit for Christ to be formed in us.

In Galatians 4:19 Paul expresses his concern for this growth in Christ: "My little children . . . I labor in birth again until Christ is formed in you." With a pastor's heart, Paul uses this descriptive language to express both his love ("My little children") and his longing (that Christ be "formed in you"). This involved "labor in birth again." The apostle had experienced this anguish when he brought these Galatians to birth through the Holy Spirit in the first instance. But once again he travails in the Spirit to bring them to maturity in Christ. "Paul was not only a prince of evangelists; he was also a prince of pastors." He knew that "the perfecting by the Spirit" would not be complete until his converts took "the shape of Christ" (NEB).

How tragically this is lacking in our churches! Easy believism is taking its toll, not only with statistics but with souls. Where are the godly men and women who travail in prayerful preaching and teaching to bring about genuine maturity in Christ? No doubt this *passion* for souls was Paul's *purpose* for souls. He writes to the Colossians, "I now rejoice in my sufferings for you, and fill up in my flesh what is lacking in the afflictions of Christ, for the sake of His body, which is the church, of which I became a minister according to the stewardship from God which was given to me for you, to fulfill the word of God, the mystery which has been hidden from ages and from generations, but now has been revealed to His saints. To them God willed to make known what are the riches of the glory of this mystery among the Gentiles: which is Christ in you, the hope of glory. Him we preach, warning every man and teaching every man in all wisdom, that we may present every man perfect in Christ Jesus" (Col. 1:24-28).

I want to underscore another point. The Holy Spirit not only originates the life of Christ in us, consolidates the life of Christ in us, but in the third place *the Holy Spirit authenticates the life of Christ in us:* "He . . . supplies the Spirit . . . and works miracles" (Gal. 3:5). This could be translated "miracles," as in Mark 6:2; 1 Cor. 12:10; or "miraculous powers," as in 1 Cor. 12:6; Phil. 2:13; Eph. 2:2. To illustrate this, the apostle zeros in on a perfect model. He cites Abraham who "believed God, and it was accounted to him for righteousness" (Gal. 3:6). While the apostle proceeds with a detailed interpretation of the Genesis texts, I will limit the illustration to our immediate application.

How does the Spirit authenticate the life of Christ in you and me? To answer that question fully would involve a complete study of this great "father of the faithful." The key word for our purpose is *miracle.*

There was, first of all, *the miracle of FAITH.* Abraham "believed God" (Gal. 3:6; see also Rom. 4:5). Although Abraham came from a family of idol worshipers (Josh. 24:2, 14) in Ur of the Chaldees, he responded to God's call to migrate to the land of Canaan. The fact that God revealed Himself to Abraham is repeatedly stated in the Genesis account (see especially Gen. 12:3; 18:18; 26:4; 28:14).

But the astonishing statement of our Lord during His earthly life clinches the miracle of faith in Abraham's life. Jesus declared, "Your father Abraham rejoiced to see My day, and he saw it and was glad" (John 8:56). The patriarch is mentioned forty times in the Old Testament and some seventy times in the New Testament, but this statement of Jesus is crucial. Dr. George R. Beasley-Murray explains:

> In Jewish terminology, "the day" usually signifies the appearance of the Messiah in the last days, but here [John 8:56], as in the Gospel generally, it [denotes] the ministry of Jesus in its totality as Revealer and Redeemer, through which the saving sovereignty of God comes. . . . Abraham, seeing the day of salvation as the day of Jesus, acknowledged that the Son of God-Redeemer, not himself, was the means of bringing to pass the divine purpose for blessing the nations. . . . The verb is expressive, "he was overjoyed!"[4]

And our text tells us that "Abraham 'believed God, and it was accounted to him for righteousness'" (Gal. 3:6; see also Gen. 15:6). Here was the miracle of faith by the power of the Spirit.

Second, there was *the miracle of FRUIT.* "Therefore know that only those who are of faith are sons of Abraham. And the Scripture, foreseeing that God would justify the nations by faith, preached the gospel to Abraham beforehand, saying, 'In you all the nations shall be blessed.' So then those who are of faith are blessed with believing Abraham" (Gal. 3:7-9). Through Abraham God has blessed the nations of the earth (study Gen. 15; note v. 5). And Paul declares it right here in our text where he affirms, "Those who are of faith are blessed with believing Abraham" (Gal. 3:9).

This is how the Spirit of God authenticates the life of Christ in us. First it is FAITH, then it is FRUIT. This is the miracle of the Christian life. Whatever else is said about miraculous powers, nothing supersedes the miracle of faith and fruit wrought in us by the Holy Spirit. This is what the indwelling life of Jesus is all about.

Nowhere in the New Testament is this more gloriously expressed than in Paul's revealing prayer in Ephesians 3:14-21:

> For this reason I bow my knees to the Father of our Lord Jesus Christ, from whom the whole family in heaven and earth is named, that He would grant you, according to the riches of His glory, to be strengthened with might through His Spirit in the inner man, that Christ may dwell in your hearts through *faith;* that you, being rooted and grounded in love, may be able to comprehend with all the saints what is the width and length and depth and height—to know the *love* of Christ which passes knowledge; that you may be filled with all the fullness of God. Now to Him who is able to do

exceedingly abundantly above all that we ask or think, according to the power that works in us, to Him be glory in the church by Christ Jesus throughout all ages, world without end. Amen.

Note the words *faith* and *love*. The apostle is asking the Father in heaven to strengthen the believers in Ephesus "through His Spirit in the inner man, that Christ may dwell in [their] hearts through *faith;* . . . being rooted and grounded in *love."* So how does the Holy Spirit authenticate the life of Christ in us? Clearly, by the miracle of faith and love ("The fruit of the Spirit is love" Gal. 5:22).

I remember the moment when the Spirit of God strengthened me in my inner man to discover that I could exchange my failure for "all the fullness of God" (Eph. 3:19). He opened my eyes to see that what I could not do, God could do in me and through me "exceedingly abundantly above all that [I could] ask or think, according to the power that works in [me]." Only one response is appropriate: "To Him be glory in the church by Christ Jesus throughout all ages, world without end. Amen" (Eph. 3:20–21).

Himself

> *Once it was the blessing, now it is the Lord;*
> *Once it was the feeling, now it is His Word;*
> *Once His gift I wanted, now, the Giver own;*
> *Once I sought for healing, now Himself alone.*

Once 'twas painful trying, now 'tis perfect trust;
Once a half salvation, now the uttermost;
Once 'twas ceaseless holding, now He holds me fast;
Once 'twas constant drifting, now my anchor's cast.

Once 'twas busy planning, now 'tis trustful prayer;
Once 'twas anxious caring, now He has the care;
Once 'twas what I wanted, now what Jesus says;
Once 'twas constant asking, now 'tis ceaseless praise.

Once it was my working, His it hence shall be;
Once I tried to use Him, now He uses me;
Once the pow'r I wanted, now the Mighty One;
Once for self I labored, now for Him alone.

Once I hop'd in Jesus, now I know He's mine;
Once my lamps were dying, now they brightly shine;
Once for death I waited, now His coming hail;
And my hopes are anchored safe within the veil.

All in all forever,
Jesus will I sing;
Ev'rything in Jesus,
And Jesus ev'rything.

A. B. Simpson

For Further Study

1. Why are good works or human merit insufficient either for salvation or for living the Christian life (see Ephesians 2:8-9; Galatians 3:1, 3)? What does grace accomplish that our own efforts cannot?

2. Why is it *foolish* to try to live the Christian life through self-effort (see Galatians 3:1)? Is this merely an intellectual problem or a moral one? Explain.

3. In what ways do Christian believers "neglect" salvation (see Hebrews 2:1-4)? What implications does this have for our living the Christ-life in its fullness? What can you do to avoid such neglect and drifting?

4. Why is self-effort in the Christian walk *futile* (see Galatians 3:4)? What happens when we rely on just trying harder? How is grace the solution to this dilemma?

5. How do the fruits of *trying* and of *trusting* differ (see Acts 6:4)? How has each manifested itself in your life? How can we experience the brokenness needed to bring us to a full reliance on God?

6. The Holy Spirit originates the life of Christ in us, consolidates the life of Christ in us, and authenticates the life of Christ in us (see Philippians 1:6; Galatians 3:3, 5). How are we to cooperate with the Spirit to facilitate these activities within us? Is the life of Christ evident in your life these days? What can you do to experience this more fully?

Epilogue
Faith and Love in Action

I N THE PRECEDING CHAPTERS I HAVE SOUGHT TO explain and apply the liberating message of life in Christ as embodied in Galatians 2:20. The implications as well as the ramifications in my own life would require another book. As it happens, that book has been authored already by my good friend Dr. John Phillips and is available in Christian bookstores. It is entitled *Only One Life*.[1] I mention this because of the criticism often raised by those who oppose teaching on the victorious life. They maintain that this "emphasis" is pietistic instead of activistic—but nothing could be further from the truth!

When God set me free through the study of Galatians 2:20, nothing could hold me back from serving my Lord immediately and wholeheartedly. For over fifty years I have exercised the God-given gifts of the evangelist, the preacher, the pastor, the teacher—in crusades, conventions, local churches, and more recently in institutes for the training of leaders and pastors in the art of anointed expository preaching. By preaching the Word and by means of radio, television, tapes, and videos, the message of life has been shared around the world. To the glory of God, countless thousands have come into a new experience of Christ in all His fullness and now are serving in their Jerusalems, Judeas, Samarias—even to the ends of the earth.

I put on record this simple testimony to confirm the fact that the truth expounded in this book is not quietism; it is dynamism! Jesus summed it up exquisitely when He said, "As the Father has sent Me, I also send you" (John 20:21). Just as the Lord Jesus fleshed out in His life the will of His Father by the power of the Holy Spirit, so I claim—and a multitude of others with me— that the principle of the outliving of the indwelling Christ is gloriously possible on the basis of both dependent faith and devoted love IN ACTION.

ACTION in the context of our theme verse, Galatians 2:20, requires a consideration of three important references to the crucified life that punctuate the unfolding message of this Galatian epistle (see 3:1; 5:24; 6:14). My book would be incomplete without a brief review of these pivotal passages.

ACTION Means Obedience to the Scriptures. "O foolish Galatians! Who has bewitched you that you should not *obey the truth,* before whose eyes Jesus Christ was clearly portrayed among you as *crucified?*" (Gal. 3:1; see also vv. 6–9). The grave danger that Paul is addressing here is that of experience versus doctrine. Paul had preached the gospel and had publicly portrayed Jesus Christ as *crucified.* The Galatians had believed the gospel and had received the Spirit. These were the facts of their experience. But having begun in the Spirit (who always works through the Word), they were reverting now to the works of the flesh to supplement the gospel! Paul told them in no uncertain manner that they were "foolish" and "bewitched." To depend on their works in the flesh instead of the Word and the Spirit was not advancement but "retardment." Indeed, it was degeneracy (see chapter 6, "Not I, But Christ and His Grace").

This danger is with us today. All around us are people seeking for some "new experience." Paul predicted this when he exhorted Timothy to "preach the word!" He said the time would come when people would not endure sound doctrine, but according to their own desires (emotions and feelings) would heap up for themselves teachers who would tickle their ears and satisfy their cravings (2 Tim. 4:2–3).

To be balanced in our Christian walk, we must ever move from doctrine to experience—and *never* the other way around. For this reason alone, *we must be people of the Word* (see Afterword). This means daily meditation on the Word (Ps. 1:2), daily application of the Word (John 7:17; James 1:21–25), and daily preservation by the Word (1 John 1:14; Eph. 6:14, 17). The Lord Jesus in His perfect humanity *never* missed His quiet time with the Father and with the Word (Isa. 50:4–6; Matt. 4:4; Mark 1:35). If He needed this devotional discipline to strengthen His dependence on the Spirit and to please His Father day by day, how much more do you and I! I remember Dr. Graham Scroggie once saying, "Pray when you feel like it, pray when you don't feel like it, and pray until you do feel like it!" There we have it then—obedience to the Lord and a life of prayer rather than the vacillations of the self-life.

ACTION Means Reliance on the Spirit. "Walk in the Spirit, and you shall not fulfill the lust of the flesh. . . . Those who are Christ's have *crucified* the flesh with its passions and desires" (Gal. 5:16, 24; read also 16–25). Even though we "have been crucified with Christ" (2:20), we are informed here that there is also a human responsibility. The crucifixion of the flesh in 5:24 is not something done *to* us but *by* us. It is we ourselves who are said to have "crucified the flesh." In Galatians 2:20, by faith-union with Christ, we "have been crucified"; here in 5:24 it is *we* who take action.

Initially, this happens at conversion, but day by day there is something we have to do in the power of the Spirit. The word is clear: "If you are living according to the flesh, you must die; but if by the Spirit you are putting to death the deeds of the body, you will live" (Rom. 8:13, NASB). This obviously calls for a continual reliance on the Holy Spirit. So in Galatians 5:16–25 we are exhorted to "walk in the Spirit" (v. 16). To fulfill this command we must be "led by the Spirit" (v. 18). The Spirit does the leading; we do the walking. For the Spirit to lead, He must *control*; so Paul adds, "Live in the Spirit" (v. 25). This is helpfully explained and applied in Ephesians 5:18 where we are directed to "be filled [controlled] with the Spirit." This demands disciplined reliance—the verb is in the imperative; daily reliance— the verb is in the present tense; and, most importantly, demonstrative reliance—there is Spirit-controlled worship in the church (vv. 19–21), Spirit-controlled welfare in the home (vv. 22—6:9), and Spirit-controlled warfare and witness in the world (vv. 10–20).

So ACTION means reliance on the Spirit. Only He can make Jesus real and radiant in and through our lives in the church, the home, and the world.

ACTION Means Allegiance to the Savior. "God forbid

that I should glory except in the cross of our Lord Jesus Christ, by whom the world has been crucified to me, and I to the world" (Gal. 6:14). The cross for Paul was not something to escape but something to embrace. He boasted in the cross. The fact of the matter is that we cannot boast in ourselves and in the cross at one and the same time. To boast in the cross is to declare our unquestioned allegiance to the Christ of the cross. Our love and our language must be:

> *On a hill far away stood an old rugged cross,*
> *The emblem of suffering and shame;*
> *And I love that old cross where the dearest and best*
> *For a world of lost sinners was slain.*
>
> *Oh, that old rugged cross, so despised by the world,*
> *Has a wondrous attraction for me;*
> *For the dear Lamb of God left His glory above*
> *To bear it to dark Calvary.*
>
> *In the old rugged cross, stained with blood so divine,*
> *A wondrous beauty I see;*
> *For 'twas on that old cross Jesus suffered and died*
> *To pardon and sanctify me.*
>
> *To the old rugged cross I will ever be true,*
> *Its shame and reproach gladly bear;*
> *Then He'll call me some day to my home far away,*
> *Where His glory forever I'll share.*

So I'll cherish the old rugged cross,
Till my trophies at last I lay down;
I will cling to the old rugged cross,
And exchange it some day for a crown.

George Bennard

We cannot sing those words and understand the truth of Galatians 6:14 without parting company with the world. We remain in the world until Jesus comes or calls, but we are "not of the world" (John 17:15-18). Indeed, we are solemnly warned, "Whoever . . . wants to be a friend of the world makes himself an enemy of God" (James 4:4). Our task is to preach to the world, not pander to it. The world is a society of unbelievers under satanic control (1 John 5:19). Once we were part of this system; but now we must not care what the world thinks or says of us and does to us. "The world has been crucified to [us], and [we] to the world" (6:14). Our allegiance is to Jesus Christ as Lord—now and forever!

So the message of this book is "not I, but Christ." For the committed Christian, life in Christ means obedience to the Scriptures, reliance on the Spirit, and allegiance to the Savior. The "I" of my life, your life, is now crossed out (†), and our glory is all the cross—yes, the Christ of the cross.

A girl was sent to a finishing school by her wealthy parents. There she learned science, art, dancing, and many other things. One night she went to an evangelistic meeting, and at the close of the service she accepted Christ as her own personal Savior. She gave her heart to Christ, yielded to Him, and decided she would dedicate her life to missionary service. She wrote home to her father and told him of her decision.

He went into a rage and wrote to her immediately, saying, "Get on the next plane and come home." She obeyed and returned to her home. As her father met her, he said, "I did not send you to school to get religion. That is all right for poor folk and half-wits, but not for a child in your stratum of life. You will have to get this religion out of your head. If by tomorrow morning you have not decided to give up this foolish notion of religion, you may pack your suitcase and leave this home."

She went to her room with a heavy heart. It would mean loss of love, culture, money, prestige. On her knees she fought it out. The next morning she packed her suitcase. Before leaving, she stepped over to the piano in the living room and started to play and sing:

> *Jesus, I my cross have taken,*
> *All to leave and follow Thee;*
> *Destitute, despised, forsaken,*
> *Thou, from hence, my all must be:*
> *Perish every fond ambition,*
> *All I've sought and hoped and known;*
> *Yet how rich is my condition:*
> *God and Heaven are still my own!*

She arose and, with tears streaming down her face, turned toward the door. Before she could open it, her father stepped out from behind the curtain where he had been listening to her playing and with emotion said, "Wait! I did not know that Jesus Christ meant as much to you as that. I did not know that you were willing to give up father, mother, home, and prestige just for Jesus. Daughter, forgive me. I must be beside myself. If such a great love can take hold of your heart, there must be something in it. Sit down here and tell me how I can be a Christian."[2]

From that moment it was "not I, but Christ" for father and daughter; and it must be equally so for you and me. Oh, that our constant desire and prayer might be:

Not I, but Christ, be honored, loved, exalted;
Not I, but Christ, be seen, be known, be heard;
Not I, but Christ, in every look and action;
Not I, but Christ, in every thought and word.

Not I, but Christ, to gently soothe in sorrow;
Not I, but Christ, to wipe the falling tear;
Not I, but Christ, to lift the weary burden!
Not I, but Christ, to hush away all fear.

Not I, but Christ, in lowly, silent labor;
Not I, but Christ, in humble, earnest toil;
Christ, only Christ! no show, no ostentation!
Christ, none but Christ, the gatherer of the spoil.

Christ, only Christ, ere long will fill my vision;
Glory excelling, soon, full soon, I'll see—
Christ, only Christ, my every wish fulfilling—
Christ, only Christ, my All in all to be.

Oh, to be saved from myself, dear Lord,
Oh, to be lost in Thee;
Oh, that it may be no more I,
But Christ that lives in me.

A. A. Whiddington

For Further Study

1. Why is it imperative that we be people of the Word (see Psalm 1:2; John 7:17; James 1:21-25; 1 John 1:14; Ephesians 6:14, 17)? Why is it important that we move from doctrine to experience and never the other way around? What happens in your life when you fail to spend time regularly in the Scriptures?

2. Compare Galatians 2:20 and 5:24. Do we crucify the flesh ourselves, or is it done to us by another? What is God's part in this, and what is ours? What is the significance of all this?

3. In what sense are we to embrace and boast about the cross of Christ (see Galatians 6:14)? What does this do to self-boasting? How can we declare our allegiance to Christ day by day?

Daily Communion with God

DAILY COMMUNION WITH GOD IS MORE THAN A commendable practice; it is absolutely vital to a life of sustained spirituality and maturity. It is the barometer of the Christian life. Jesus said, "Man shall not live by bread alone, but by every word that proceeds from the mouth of God" (Matt. 4:4). Read that without the negative comparison, and you will see what man is to live on. "Man shall live by every spoken word that comes from God." That is not the Bible memorized, nor the Bible on your bookshelf, nor in your study. It is the word that God speaks to your soul in the quiet place of prayer and meditation. That is how man lives. You can be doctrinally correct and yet be spiritually dead. The thing that maintains life is the living Word of God spoken to your soul every day. The quiet time is vital to spiritual health, whether you are newly converted or a mature Christian (see 1 Pet. 2:2; Heb. 5:14).

The quiet time is vital for *spiritual cleansing*. You are initially cleansed by the precious blood, and again and again you have to return to the cross for restoration. But the day-to-day cleansing is from the laver of the Word (see Ps. 119:9; John 15:3; 17:17).

The quiet time is also vital to *spiritual counsel*. You can never know the true principles that determine a life of holiness and righteousness without letting "the word of Christ dwell in you richly" (see Col. 3:16; Ps. 73:24).

The quiet time is likewise vital in equipping you for *spiritual conflict.* The supreme example is our Lord Jesus Christ when He encountered Satan in the wilderness. For forty days and nights He had fed His soul on the book of Deuteronomy, and He could therefore make His sword thrusts from a personal experience of the written Word. Paul later exhorted the Ephesian believers to "take . . . the sword of the Spirit, which is the word of God" (Eph. 6:17). Important as these things are, the greatest incentive to having a daily quiet time is not your need—great as that is—but the fact that God wants to meet with you. Therefore, it is not merely a duty; it is a privilege and an honor. God in Christ has a definite time and place for meeting with you. His heart is saddened when you fail to keep the appointment. He longs, as He did with the woman of Samaria, to drink afresh of your love, devotion, and worship (see John 4:23, 24).

Establishing your quiet time is never easy. I confess quite frankly that it is harder for me to have my quiet time now than it was when I was first converted. The reason for this is that what counts *costs.*

You will find that the most vicious attacks of the adversary will be directed toward robbing you of that daily time with your Lord. And you will have to guard it fearlessly if you are to keep it. Whatever your sphere of service—as a pastor, Sunday school teacher, missionary, or Christian in the office or home—I give you little hope of living victoriously unless you are successful in maintaining your quiet time.

With the reasons for the daily quiet time, there are some practical and specific requirements. First, you will need a definite place and time. Consider the example of the Lord Jesus (see Mark 1:35). Next, have a good-sized Bible, one with print you do not have to strain to read. Don't get in the habit of waking up in the morning, rolling over in bed, and with sleepy eyes trying to read a Bible with small print. Don't stay in bed at all! Get up and wash your face or take a shower so that you are fully alert.

Another essential is a prayer list or prayer cycle—something to keep reminding you to emphasize a different request for each day. My wife and I use one that works this way:

Monday: *M* is for missionaries.

Tuesday: *T* is for thanksgiving for wonderful answers to prayer.

Wednesday: *W* is for workers.

Thursday: *T* is for tasks—our job at the church or the ministry God has given us.

Friday: *F* is for our families.

Saturday: *S* is for the saints—especially young Christians, that Christ might be formed in them.

Sunday: *S* is for sinners—in particular, the gospel services for which we are responsible.

Then you should have a quiet-time notebook or journal. I believe that the thoughts of every quiet time should be written down, even if only in brief sentence form. God gives you some-

NOT I, BUT CHRIST

thing there you'll never find in a commentary or anywhere else, and the thoughts are worth keeping.

Along with these tangible items of equipment, be sure to come to your quiet time with a spirit of expectancy. I believe such expectancy has at least three contributing factors. First of all, there is the *physical* factor. You cannot go to bed at all hours of the night and expect to get up fresh in the morning. Going to bed when you ought takes discipline, and some of these social occasions that you enjoy may be great, but they are not as precious or vital as your quiet time.

There's a *moral* factor, too, in this matter of expectancy. "If I regard iniquity in my heart, the Lord will not hear" (Ps. 66:18). When there is something in your life that is out of adjustment with the will of God, don't expect to have fellowship with Him. If you have something against another person, leave your gift at the altar and first be reconciled to that individual (Matt. 5:23–24).

Then there is a *spiritual* factor involved in this matter of expectancy. John 7:17 states, "If anyone wants to do His will, he shall know concerning the doctrine"; that is, he shall know the teaching. Revelation and obedience are like parallel lines: as you obey, so He reveals; when you cease to obey, He ceases to reveal. My experience has been this: when I find it impossible to "get through" to God, when the Bible has become a dead book to me, usually it is because there was an issue of obedience on which I had not followed through. Therefore, before proceeding with my quiet time, I have to get right with God.

Having considered the reasons and the requirements for

the quiet time, let me share some simple rules that can help you in your daily time with God.

1. The first rule is waiting. Samuel Chadwick once said, "Hurry is the death of prayer." You can get more from the Lord in five unhurried minutes than in thirty-five minutes with your eye constantly on the clock.

2. Hush yourself in God's presence. Wait until the glory of His presence seems to come upon you. Seek the power of concentration. Seek cleansing. Seek the illumination of the Holy Spirit. Above all, seek to consciously come into His presence.

3. From waiting, go on to read the Word of God and the specific passage set aside for that day. I believe with George Mueller that you can never pray aright until He has spoken to you from His Word. Avoid the "lucky dip" approach to Bible reading. Such a practice is an insult to the sacredness of the Scriptures. Read the portion at least three times: first, to discover what is there generally; next, to peruse it for what is there specifically; and then study it for what is there personally.

4. Move from reading to reflection. As you meditate on the passage in the presence of God, ask yourself: Is there any command to obey? Is there any promise to claim? Is there any new thought to follow and pursue? Is there any sin to avoid? Is there any new thought about God, about the Lord Jesus, about the Holy Spirit, about the devil? Seek to discover what God is saying to you from the passage you have read.

5. From thinking, go on to what I call recording. Take that notebook that you keep just for your quiet time and jot down briefly what the Lord has said to you. Always make it personal

and devotional. Write down the thoughts so that it will be a message to your soul.

6. Now pray. Praying has three aspects in your quiet time. First, there is adjustment. Take the message the Lord has given you—the message recorded briefly in your quiet time notebook—and pray it back to Him. That is one way of keeping your prayers alive and fresh. Pray it back until God's will becomes your will in relation to the particular message He has spoken to you. Then adore Him. Pour out your soul to Him. Thank Him. Think of His majesty, His glory and mercy. Revel in the sunshine of His presence. Talk as a child to his father, as a servant to a kind master. And listen as a lover to his beloved. Only then do you come to present your requests for yourself and to intercede for others.

7. Next, share God's message to you today with somebody else. What you share, you keep. The manna God's people gathered every day had to be shared and eaten. When it was hoarded, it bred worms and stank. You can always tell the person who merely hoards what he gets in his quiet time.

8. Most important of all, obey. Get up from your knees and say, "Lord Jesus, as I face this day, I ask You, by the power of Your indwelling Spirit, to give me the grace to put into action what You have told me to do this morning." Then go out determined to obey.

God's best for you is closely linked with this daily meeting with Him. The barometer of your Christian life can be observed by the attention you give to your quiet time each day. You cannot tell me you have surrendered to God, that

Jesus Christ is Lord of your life, or that you know the fullness of the Holy Spirit unless you have your manna in the morning.[1] May your prayer be:

> *Help me, O Lord, Thy Word to read,*
> *Upon the living Bread to feed,*
> *Seeking Thy Spirit's quickening lead*
> *That I may please Thee in all things.*

Stephen F. Olford

Appendix A

Gerald Hawthorne concludes his book with this warning:

> The Holy Spirit of God must never be thought of as a genie whose presence and power is available for personal enrichment or aggrandizement. When Jesus had been led into the desert, the arena of testing, by the Spirit and was tempted to use the power of the Spirit that was available to him to change stones into bread to satisfy his own real hunger, he refused to do so. Why? Because he knew that the power that filled him was power to do the Father's will, not his own will. It was power to equip him to triumphantly complete the mission God had given him to do, even if that involved hunger, not to prove to anyone, especially the devil, that he could perform the spectacular.
>
> Much later when Simon the magician saw the signs and great miracles performed by Philip and the other apostles through the power of the Spirit, he came with money in his hands, saying, "Give me also this power, that any one on whom I lay my hands may receive the Holy Spirit." But he was sternly rebuffed by Peter for such an iniquitously selfish desire to manipulate the Spirit for his own gain (Acts 8:9-23).
>
> The Holy Spirit is God present and active in the lives of Jesus' followers—not to make life rich and comfortable for them, but to equip them to fulfill God's mission for them in the world. It is a mission of helping, serving, healing, restor-

ing, giving, sharing, and loving—a mission of binding up the broken, of being just and striving for justice, of proclaiming the Good News that God is King, of taking the Gospel everywhere, preaching the message that God has acted to save the world and transform people in and through the life, death, and resurrection of his Son Jesus Christ.[1]

Appendix B

Dr. Alan Cole observes that Galatians 2:20 "is not so much an exhortation to personal sanctification as a powerful argument for the total sufficiency and efficacy of the work of Christ. It is true that it deals with the great motives for Christian service, but the central thought is the complete breach with the old ways of thought that is demanded by faith-committal to Christ."[1]

Appendix C

In his critique of various versions of the Bible, Dr. John R. Kohlenberger III draws attention to the fact that "the most criticized word choice in the NIV is the rendering of the Greek word *sarx* as 'sinful nature' (twenty-five times, including Romans 7:5, 18, 25), a rendering incompatible with several denominational perspectives. Many wish the NIV had stuck with the traditional and theological neutral 'flesh' and offered 'sinful nature' in its footnotes instead of the other way around."[1]

Appendix D

"Obligation" is the keynote. Only the negative side is stated; the positive side—that we are debtors to the Spirit—must be inferred. If we do not have an obligation to live in terms of the sinful nature, the conclusion must be that our obligation is to live and serve God in terms of the Spirit. It is tremendously important to grasp the import of verse 12 [Romans 8] because it teaches beyond all question that the believer still has the sinful nature within himself despite having been crucified with Christ. The flesh has not been eradicated. But we are obliged not "to live according to it." There is really no option, for the flesh is linked to death as life is linked to the Spirit. Sanctification is not a luxury but a necessity. As Bishop Handley Moule stated, "It is not an ambition; it is a duty" (in loc.). Life in accordance with the flesh is doomed to suffer death (cf. v. 6). The solicitations of the fleshly nature are constant; hence the necessity of continually putting to death (that is the force of the verb) the deeds of the body. Here "body" is equivalent to "the flesh" as in 6:6.

Though this may seem to give a negative emphasis to the life of sanctification, it should be emphasized that this is only part of the divine plan. The positive is just as important—the putting on of the Lord Jesus in such complete preoccupation with him and his will that the believer does not make provision for the flesh (cf. 13:14). Yet since the Spirit is the Spirit of life, he cannot do otherwise than oppose the flesh and its desires, the things that lead inevitably to death.[1]

Endnotes

INTRODUCTION

1. David B. Barrett, ed., *World Christian Encyclopedia: A Comparative Study of Churches and Religion in the Modern World A.D.* 1900-2000 (Nairobi, Kenya: Oxford University Press, 1982), p. v.

2. Dean M. Kelley, *Why Conservative Churches Are Growing* (New York: Harper & Row, 1972), p. 1.

3. Gordon D. Fee, *God's Empowering Presence: The Holy Spirit in the Letters of Paul* (Peabody, Mass.: Hendrickson Publishers, Inc., 1994), p. 374.

4. Gerald F. Hawthorne, *The Presence and the Power: The Significance of the Holy Spirit in the Life and Ministry of Jesus* (Dallas: Word, Inc., 1991), pp. 235, 238.

5. V. Raymond Edman, *They Found the Secret: Twenty Transformed Lives That Reveal a Touch of Eternity* (Grand Rapids: Zondervan Publishing House, 1960, 1984), pp. 151–153.

CHAPTER ONE—NOT I, BUT CHRIST

1. *F. B. Meyer Devotional Commentary* (Wheaton, Ill.: Tyndale House Publishers, Inc., 1989), p. 542.

2. Martin Luther, *A Commentary on St. Paul's Epistle to the Galatians,* rev. and completed translation based on the 'Middleton' edition of the English version of 1575 (Cambridge: James Clarke & Co. Ltd, 1953), p. 101.

3. John Stott, *The Message of Galatians* (Downers Grove, Ill.: InterVarsity Press, 1968), p. 62.

4. F. B. Meyer, *The Christ-Life for the Self-Life* (Chicago: Moody Press, n.d.), pp. 45–46.

5. William Barclay, *The Letters to the Galatians and Ephesians,* The Daily Study Bible (Edinburgh: Saint Andrew Press, 1959), pp. 23–24.

6. Percy L. Parker, ed., *Journals of John Wesley* (Chicago: Moody Press, 1974), p. 64.

7. V. Raymond Edman, *They Found the Secret: Twenty Transformed Lives That Reveal a Touch of Eternity* (Grand Rapids: Zondervan Publishing House, 1960, 1984), p. xv.

8. Walter Elwell, Foreword to ibid., pp. x–xi.

9. "John Bunyan: The Unchained Life," ibid., pp. 18–20.

10. "Handley C. G. Moule: The Fragrant Life," ibid., (1963 printing), pp. 90–92.

11. "Charles G. Trumbull: The Victorious Life," ibid., pp. 115–120.

CHAPTER TWO—NOT I, BUT CHRIST AND HIS DEATH

1. *The Wycliffe Bible Commentary* (Chicago: Moody Press, 1962), pp. 1505–6.

2. F. F. Bruce, *The Epistle of Paul to the Romans,* Tyndale New Testament Commentaries (Grand Rapids: Wm. B. Eerdmans Publishing Co., 1963), p. 155.

3. Reginald Wallis, "What Is the Deeper Meaning of the Cross?" *The New Life* (London: Pickering & Inglis Ltd., n.d.), p. 45.

4. Kenneth S. Wuest, *Galatians in the Greek New Testament* (Grand Rapids: Wm. B. Eerdmans Publishing Co., 1944), p. 81.

5. James Montgomery Boice, Galatians, *The Expositor's Bible Commentary,* ed. Frank E. Gaebelein and J. D. Douglas, Regency Reference Library (Grand Rapids: Zondervan Publishing House, 1976), 10:495, adapted.

6. Related by a missionary at Duke Street Baptist Church, Richmond, Surrey, England, while Stephen Olford was the senior pastor.

7. Leonard Ravenhill, *Why Revival Tarries* (Minneapolis: Bethany Fellowship, 1959), p. 173.

8. Dietrich Bonhoeffer, *The Cost of Discipleship,* 2nd ed. (New York: Macmillan, 1959), p. 7.

9. *Windows in Words: Illustrations and Pen-Pictures* used by Harold P. Barker (London: Pickering & Inglis Ltd., 1954), p. 43.

CHAPTER THREE—NOT I, BUT CHRIST AND HIS LIFE

1. Everett F. Harrison, Romans, *The Expositor's Bible Commentary,* ed. Frank E. Gaebelein and J. D. Douglas, Regency Reference Library (Grand Rapids: Zondervan Publishing House, 1976), 10:92.

2. H. C. G. Moule, *Ephesian Studies* (London: Hodder & Stoughton, n.d.), pp. 136–137.

3. Martin Luther, *A Commentary on St. Paul's Epistle to the Galatians,* trans. Theodore Graebner (Grand Rapids: Zondervan Publishing House, n.d.), pp. 40–41.

4. J. C. Pollock, *The Keswick Story* (London: Hodder & Stoughton, 1964), pp. 102–3.

5. Ibid., pp. 103–4.

6. Moule, *Ephesian Studies,* p. 130.

7. Ibid.

8. Charles Colson, *The Body* (Dallas, Tex.: Word, Inc., 1992), p. 304.

9. Arthur Bennett, ed., *The Valley of Vision: A Collection of Puritan Prayers and Quotations* (Carlisle, Penn.: The Banner of Truth Trust, 1975), p. 181.

CHAPTER FOUR—NOT I, BUT CHRIST AND HIS FAITH

1. Marvin R. Vincent, *Word Studies in the New Testament: Galatians,* 1887, reprint ed. (Grand Rapids: Wm. B. Eerdmans Publishing Co., 1946), p. 108.

2. Fred Mitchell, "Summary and Prospect," in *The Keswick Week, 1948* (London: Marshall, Morgan & Scott, Ltd., 1948), p. 194.

3. F. B. Meyer, *Five "Musts" of the Christian Life* (Chicago: Moody Press, 1927), p. 44.

4. Article and hymn by A. B. Simpson reprinted by kind permission of Christian Publications, Inc., Camp Hill, Penn.

5. W. E. Vine, et al., *Vine's Expository Dictionary of Biblical Words,* New Testament Section (Nashville: Thomas Nelson Publishers, 1985), p. 222.
6. Will H. Houghton in *The Living Christ.* Quoted in *3000 Illustrations for Christian Service,* Walter B. Knight, comp. (Grand Rapids: Wm. B. Eerdmans Publishing Co., 1952), p. 252.
7. W. Harold Mare, 1 Corinthians, *The Expositor's Bible Commentary,* ed. Frank E. Gaebelein and J. D. Douglas, Regency Reference Library (Grand Rapids: Zondervan Publishing House, 1978), 10:270.

CHAPTER SIX—NOT I, BUT CHRIST AND HIS GRACE

1. J. C. Macaulay, *Expository Commentary on Hebrews* (Chicago: Moody Press, 1948), pp. 26–27.
2. Archibald Naismith, ed., *2400 Outlines, Notes, Quotes & Anecdotes* (Grand Rapids: Baker Book House, 1991), p. 162, adapted.
3. Ibid.
4. George R. Beasley-Murray, *Word Biblical Commentary* [John], vol. 36 (Dallas: Word, Inc., 1987), p. 138.

EPILOGUE—FAITH AND LOVE IN ACTION

1. John Phillips, *Only One Life* (Neptune, N.J.: Loizeaux Brothers, Inc., 1994).
2. "Taking Up the Cross," *The Prairie Overcomer,* January 1956, 29:20–21.

AFTERWORD—DAILY COMMUNION WITH GOD

1. Adapted from Stephen Olford's booklet, *Manna in the Morning,* pp. 1–13. Read also his booklet, *Becoming a Man of God.* Both available from Encounter Ministries, Inc., P.O. Box 757800, Memphis, Tenn. 38175-7800.

APPENDIX A

1. Gerald F. Hawthorne, *The Presence and the Power: The Significance of the Holy Spirit in the Life and Ministry of Jesus* (Dallas: Word, Inc., 1991), pp. 242–43.

APPENDIX B

1. Alan Cole, *Tyndale New Testament Commentaries: Galatians* (Grand Rapids: Wm. B. Eerdmans Publishing Co., 1965) p. 82.

APPENDIX C

1. John R. Kohlenberger III, review, "A Summary Critique: The Message," *Christian Research Journal* (Spring/Summer 1994): 43.

APPENDIX D

1. Everett F. Harrison, Romans, *The Expositor's Bible Commentary,* ed. Frank E. Gaebelein and J. D. Douglas, Regency Reference Library (Grand Rapids: Zondervan Publishing House, 1976), 10:92.

Bibliography

Allen, R. Earl. *Bible Paradoxes*. Grand Rapids: Baker Book House, 1963.

Arthur, Kay. *Cleansing and Filling: A Guide to Fellowship with God and a Life of Power in the Holy Spirit*. Chattanooga, Tenn.: Precept Ministries of Reach Out, Inc., 1991.

Bangley, Bernard. *Growing in His Image*. A reinterpretation of the great devotional classic *The Imitation of Christ* by Thomas à Kempis. Wheaton, Ill.: Harold Shaw Publishers, 1983.

Barabas, Steven. *So Great Salvation: The History and Message of the Keswick Convention*. London: Marshall, Morgan & Scott, 1952.

Barclay, Ian. *Down with Heaven: Living Out the Fruit of the Spirit*. London: Church Pastoral Aid Society, 1975.

Barker, John H. J. *This Is the Will of God: A Study in the Doctrine of Entire Sanctification as a Definite Experience*. London: The Epworth Press, 1954.

Baxter, J. Sidlow. *A Series of Devotional Studies in Knowing, Loving, and Serving Our Lord Jesus Christ*. Grand Rapids: Zondervan Publishing House, 1959.

Beet, J. Agar. *The New Life in Christ: A Study in Personal Religion*. London: Hodder & Stoughton, n.d.

Bell, L. Nelson. *Convictions to Live By*. Grand Rapids: Wm. B. Eerdmans Publishing Co., 1966.

Bennett, Richard A. *Food for Faith*. Revised and expanded. Victor, Colo.: Trumpet House Publishers, 1994.

Berkouwer, G. C. *Faith and Sanctification: Studies in Dogmatics.* Grand Rapids: Wm. B. Eerdmans Publishing Co., 1952.

Bonar, Horatius. *God's Way of Holiness.* Chicago: Moody Press, n.d.

Bonhoeffer, Dietrich. *The Cost of Discipleship,* rev. ed. New York: Macmillan, 1949.

Bostwick, C. F. *What Is the New Life?* Vineland, N.J.: New Life Books, Inc., 1975.

Bourne, F. W. *All for Christ, Christ for All.* London: Bible Christian Book Room, n.d.

Brengle, S. L. *The Way of Holiness.* The Warrior's Library, no. 5, 4th ed. London: The Salvation Army Book Department, 1904.

Briscoe, D. Stuart. *Getting into God: Practical Guidelines to the Christian Life.* Special crusade ed. prepared for the Billy Graham Evangelistic Association, Minneapolis, Minn. Grand Rapids: Zondervan Corporation, 1975.

_____. *Spirit Life: Living, Loving, Learning . . . and Growing in the Lord.* Old Tappan, N.J.: Fleming H. Revell, 1983.

_____. *The Fullness of Christ.* Grand Rapids: Zondervan Publishing House, 1965.

Cable, Mildred, and Francesca French. *Towards Spiritual Maturity: A Book for Those Who Seek It.* London: Hodder & Stoughton, 1939.

Chadwick, W. F. P. *The Inner Life.* London: The Canterbury Press, 1946.

Chambers, Oswald. *Approved unto God.* London: Simpkin Marshall Ltd., reprinted 1948.

_____. *Disciples Indeed.* London: Marshall, Morgan & Scott, 1955.

_____. *If Thou Wilt Be Perfect: Talks on Spiritual Philosophy.* London: Simpkin Marshall Ltd., n.d.

Chapman, Robert C. *Choice Sayings.* London: Marshall, Morgan & Scott, n.d.

Coleman, William L. *The Pharisees' Guide to Total Holiness.* Minneapolis: Bethany House Publishers, 1977.

Collins, Marjorie A. *Dedication: What It's All About—How to Completely Dedicate Yourself to Christ and Follow Through on That Commitment.* Minneapolis: Bethany House Publishers, 1976.

Cosgrove, Jr., Francis M. *Essentials of New Life: Biblical Truths a New Christian Needs to Know.* Colorado Springs, Colo.: NavPress, 1978.

Crane, J. T. *Holiness: The Birthright of all God's Children.* Arlington, Tex.: Nelson & Phillips, 1874.

Dieter, Melvin E., Anthony A. Hoekema, Stanley M. Horton, J. Robertson McQuilkin, and John Walvoord. *Five Views on Sanctification.* Grand Rapids: Zondervan Publishing House, 1987.

Duewel, Wesley L. *Ablaze for God.* Grand Rapids: Francis Asbury Press of Zondervan Publishing House, 1989.

_____. *Measure Your Life: 17 Ways to Evaluate Your Life from God's Perspective.* Academic and Professional Books. Grand Rapids: Zondervan Publishing House, 1992.

Duncan, George. *Marks of Christian Maturity: Becoming the Kind of Christian God Wants You to Be.* Basingstoke, Hants., England: Pickering & Inglis, 1986.

Dunn, Ronald. *Any Christian Can! Living in Victory.* Kalamazoo, Mich.: Master's Press, Inc., 1973.

Edman, V. Raymond. *The Disciplines of Life.* Wheaton, Ill.: Van Kampen Press, n.d.

_____. *They Found the Secret.* Grand Rapids: Zondervan Publishing House, 1960, 1984.

Ferrin, Howard W. *Living Above: Messages, Songs and Poems,* 2d ed. Grand Rapids: Zondervan Publishing House, 1942.

Finney, Charles G. *Victory Over the World* (revival messages). Grand Rapids: Kregel Publications, 1966.

Flynn, Leslie B. *Me Be Like Jesus?* Wheaton, Ill.: Victor Books, a div. of Scripture Press Publications, Inc., 1974.

Goodman, George. *I Live; Yet Not I or God's Open Secret of Liberty from the Guilt, Reign and Fruit of Sin.* London: Pickering & Inglis, n.d.

Gordon, A. J. *In Christ or The Believer's Union with His Lord.* Grand Rapids: Baker Book House, 1964.

Green, Michael. *New Life, New Lifestyle.* London: Hodder & Stoughton, 1973.

Grubb, Norman P. *God Unlimited.* London: Lutterworth Press, 1962.

_____. *The Deep Things of God.* London: Lutterworth Press, 1958.

Guthrie, Malcolm. *Learning to Live.* London: Marshall, Morgan & Scott, 1955.

Havergal, Frances Ridley. *Kept for the Master's Use.* London: Nisbet & Co. Ltd., n.d.

Hopkins, Evan Henry. *The Law of Liberty in the Spiritual Life.* London: Marshall, Morgan & Scott, 1952.

Hopkins, Hugh Evan. *Henceforth: The Meaning of Christian Discipleship.* Downers Grove, Ill.: InterVarsity Press, 1942, 1964.

Huegel, F. J. *Bone of His Bone.* London: Marshall, Morgan & Scott, n.d.

Hutchings, Eric. *Training for Triumph in Victorious Living.* Grand Rapids: Zondervan Publishing House, 1959.

Jones, E. Stanley. *Victorious Living.* London: Hodder & Stoughton, 1936.

Jones, Jim C. *Look Inside.* Atlanta, Ga.: Crossroads Publications, Inc., 1974.

Ketcham, Robert T. *God's Provision for Normal Christian Living.* Chicago: Moody Press, 1960.

Kuyper, Abraham. *The Practice of Godliness.* Grand Rapids: Wm. B. Eerdmans Publishing Co., 1948.

Lambert, D. M. *Still Higher for His Highest: Devotional Selections for Every Day by Oswald Chambers.* Grand Rapids: Zondervan Publishing House, 1970.

Langston, E. L. *Glorious Victory*. London: Marshall, Morgan & Scott, n.d.

Lawson, J. Gilchrist. *Deeper Experiences of Famous Christians*. Anderson, Ind.: The Warner Press, 1911.

Lewis, F. Warburton. *The Unseen Life*. London: H. R. Allenson, 1894.

Loizeaux, A. S. *Christian Joy*. New York: Loizeaux Brothers, Inc., n.d.

MacDonald, George. *Creation in Christ*. From the three volumes of *Unspoken Sermons*, 1870, 1885, 1891. Ed. Rolland Hein. Wheaton, Ill.: Harold Shaw Publishers, 1976.

MacDonald, Thomas. *Discovering Our High Calling*. Brooklyn: Bible Christian Union, 1967.

MacNeil, John. *The Spirit-filled Life and Other Messages*. London: Marshall, Morgan & Scott, n.d.

Mantle, J. Gregory. *The Way of the Cross: A Contribution to the Doctrine of Christian Sanctity*. London: Marshall Brothers Ltd., 1896.

Matthews, Victor M. *Personal Success: The Promise of God*. Grand Rapids: Diadem Productions, Inc., 1970.

Maxwell, L. E. *Abandoned to Christ*. Grand Rapids: Wm. B. Eerdmans Publishing Co., 1955.

_____. *Born Crucified*. Chicago: Moody Press, 1945.

_____. *Crowded to Christ*. Grand Rapids: Wm. B. Eerdmans Publishing Co., 1950.

McConkey, James H. *The Surrendered Life: Victory Through Obedience*. Special abridged edition. Ed. Earl O. Roe. Kalamazoo, Mich.: Master's Press, Inc, 1977.

_____. *The Way of Victory: A Series of Studies upon Victory over Sin*. Pittsburgh: Silver Publishing Society, 1937.

McDonald, W. *Scriptural Way of Holiness*. London: Richard D. Dickinson, 1883.

McLaughlin, Raymond W., et al. *Drastic Discipleship and Other Expository*

Sermons. Evangelical Pulpit Library. Grand Rapids: Baker Book House, 1963.

Meyer, F. B. *The Christ-Life for the Self-Life.* Chicago: Moody Press, n.d.

———. *Five "Musts" of the Christian Life.* Chicago: Moody Press, 1927.

———. *Saved and Kept: Counsels to Young Believers and Christian Endeavourers.* London: Morgan & Scott Ltd., n.d.

Morgan, G. Campbell. *Discipleship.* London: Allenson & Co. Ltd., n.d.

———. *The Simple Things of the Christian Life.* London: Westminster City Publishing Co. Ltd., n.d.

Moule, H. C. G. *Thoughts on Union with Christ.* London: Seeley & Co., 1886.

Murray, Andrew. *Abide in Christ: Thoughts on the Blessed Life of Fellowship with the Son of God.* London: James Nisbet & Co., 1885.

———. *The Inner Chamber.* Contemporized by Leona F. Choy. Ft. Washington, Penn.: Christian Literature Crusade, n.d.

Murray, John. *The Daily Life of the Christian.* London: SCM Press, Ltd., 1955.

———, ed. *Wholly for God: Selections from the Writings of William Law.* Minneapolis: Bethany House Publishers, 1976. Reproduced from the 1894 edition published by James Nisbet & Co., London.

Nee, Watchman [pseud.]. *The Normal Christian Life.* Ft. Washington, Penn.: Christian Literature Crusade, 1957.

———. *The Release of the Spirit.* Cloverdale, Ind.: Sure Foundation for Ministry of Life, 1965.

Needham, David C. *Birthright: Christian, Do You Know Who You Are?* Portland, Ore.: Multnomah Press, 1979.

Olford, Stephen F. *Going Places with God.* Wheaton, Ill.: Victor Books, a div. of Scripture Press Publications, Inc., 1983.

Packer, J. I. *Knowing God.* Downers Grove, Ill.: InterVarsity Press, 1973.

_____. *A Quest for Godliness: The Puritan Vision of the Christian Life.* Wheaton, Ill.: Crossway Books, 1990.

Paxson, Ruth. *Life on the Highest Plane: A Study of the Spiritual Nature and Needs of Man.* Chicago: Moody Press, 1928.

_____. *Rivers of Living Water: How Obtained—How Maintained: Studies Setting Forth the Believer's Possessions in Christ.* London: Marshall, Morgan & Scott, 1930.

Pentecost, J. Dwight. *Pattern for Christian Maturity: Conduct and Conflict in the Christian Life.* Chicago: Moody Press, 1966.

Peterson, Eugene H. *A Long Obedience in the Same Direction: Discipleship in an Instant Society.* Downers Grove, Ill.: InterVarsity Press, 1980.

Piper, John. *Desiring God: Meditations of a Christian Hedonist.* Portland, Ore.: Multnomah Press, 1986.

Price, Charles W. *Alive in Christ: The Christian Life as Seen in the Ark of the Covenant.* London: Marshall Pickering, 1990.

Prior, Kenneth F. W. *The Way of Holiness: The Christian Doctrine of Sanctification.* London: Inter-Varsity Fellowship, 1967.

Raud, Elsa. *In Christ Jesus.* Brooklyn: Bible Christian Union, 1963.

Redpath, Alan. *Victorious Christian Living: Studies in the Book of Joshua.* Old Tappan, N.J.: Fleming H. Revell Co., 1955.

_____. *Victorious Christian Faith.* Old Tappan, N.J.: Fleming H. Revell Co., 1984.

Rees, Paul S. *Christian, Commit Yourself.* Old Tappan, N.J.: Fleming H. Revell Co., 1957.

_____. *If God Be for Us,* 1940 ed. Grand Rapids: Wm. B. Eerdmans Publishing Co., 1951.

Rendall, T. S. *Discipleship in Depth: What It Means to Be Christ's Disciple in the Space Age.* Three Hills, Alberta, Canada: Prairie Bible Institute, 1981.

Ryle, J. C. *Holiness: Its Nature, Hindrances, Difficulties and Roots.* London: James Clarke & Co., Ltd., 1956.

Sanders, J. Oswald. *Light on Life's Problems*. London: Marshall, Morgan & Scott, 1944.

———. *On to Maturity*. Chicago: Moody Press, 1962.

———. *Problems of Christian Discipleship*. London: China Inland Mission, n.d.

Schroeder, David E. *Follow Me: The Master Plan for Men*. Grand Rapids: Baker Book House, 1992.

See, Isaac M. *The Rest of Faith*. New York: W. C. Palmer, Jr., Women's Printing House, 1871.

Showers, Renald E. *The New Nature*. Neptune, N.J.: Loizeaux Brothers, Inc., 1986.

Smith, Hannah Whitall. *The Christian's Secret of a Happy Life*. London: Nisbet & Co. Ltd, n.d.

Stanley, Charles. *The Wonderful Spirit-Filled Life*. Nashville: Thomas Nelson Publishers, 1992.

Steer, Roger. *Spiritual Secrets of George Mueller*. Wheaton, Ill.: Harold Shaw Publishers and Robesonia, Penn.: OMF Books, 1985. First printed as *A Living Reality*. London: Hodder & Stoughton Ltd.

Taylor, Howard and Geraldine. *Hudson Taylor's Spiritual Secret*. Ed., rev. Gregg Lewis. Grand Rapids: Discovery House Publishers, 1990.

Taylor, Jack R. *Much More: A View of the Believer's Resources in Christ*. Nashville: Broadman Press, 1972.

———. *The Key to Triumphant Living: An Adventure in Personal Discovery*. Nashville: Broadman Press, 1971.

Taylor, Richard Shelley. *The Disciplined Life: Studies in the Fine Art of Christian Discipleship*. Kansas City, Mo.: Beacon Hill Press, 1962.

Thomas, W. Ian. *The Saving Life of Christ*. Grand Rapids: Zondervan Publishing House, 1961.

Torrey, R. A. *How to Succeed in the Christian Life*. Old Tappan, N.J.: Fleming H. Revell Co., 1906.

Tozer, A. W. *The Divine Conquest.* Harrisburg: Christian Publications, Inc., 1950.

_____. *The Pursuit of God.* London: Marshall, Morgan & Scott, Ltd., 1948, 1961.

_____. *The Root of the Righteous.* Harrisburg: Christian Publications, Inc., 1955.

Van Dooren, L. A. T. *The Life I Now Live: The Life of Christ Through the Holy Spirit.* Carnforth, Lancs., England: Capernwray, The Latimer Publishing Co., 1974.

Verwer, George. *Hunger for Reality.* Bromley, Kent, England: Send the Light Trust, 1972.

_____. *No Turning Back.* Wheaton, Ill.: Tyndale House Publishers, Inc., by arrangement with Hodder & Stoughton Ltd., Sevenoaks, Kent, England, 1983.

Viekman, Wm. K. *Basic Principles for Christian Growth.* Colorado Springs, Colo.: Wm. K. Viekman, 1990.

Wallis, Reginald. *The New Life: Short Simple Heart-to-Heart Talks on Practical Victory.* Glasgow: Pickering & Inglis, Ltd., n.d.

Watson, David. *Called and Committed: A World-Changing Discipleship.* Wheaton, Ill.: Harold Shaw Publishers, 1982.

Wilcox, Ethel Jones. *Power for Christian Living.* Glendale, Cal.: Gospel Light Publications, 1966.

Winter, David. *How to Walk with God.* Wheaton, Ill.: Harold Shaw Publishers, 1969.

Wright, John B. *From Sighing to Singing: A Song for the Sighing Heart.* Kalamazoo, Mich.: Master's Press, Inc., 1976.

Wyon, Olive. *On the Way: Some Reflections on the Christian Life.* Religious Book Club ed. 122. London: SCM Press, Ltd., 1958.

Young, Harry. *Roots and Wings: Making God Real in Today's World: Foundation for Belief and Encouragement to Uplifting Faith.* London: Marshall, Morgan & Scott, 1970.

General Index

Scripture Index